SAGE was founded in 1965 by Sara Miller McCune to support the dissemination of usable knowledge by publishing innovative and high-quality research and teaching content. Today, we publish over 900 journals, including those of more than 400 learned societies, more than 800 new books per year, and a growing range of library products including archives, data, case studies, reports, and video. SAGE remains majority-owned by our founder, and after Sara's lifetime will become owned by a charitable trust that secures our continued independence.

Los Angeles | London | New Delhi | Singapore | Washington DC | Melbourne

Advance Praise

Through her book, Sai takes us women on a journey that challenges the unconscious, the beliefs and the not-so-obvious in life and at the workplace. With self-reflective tools aplenty, she compels the readers to introspect, reflect and truly transform into who we can be. This book is a must-have gem for future women leaders.

Hema Ravichandar, *Strategic HR Advisor and Former Global Head HR, Infosys Technologies Limited*

SELPH—explained beautifully and in such simple articulation. In *Step Up: Women's Journey to Identity, Success and Power*, Sailaja Manacha has very succinctly presented how our history and past life build us as a person. A book that will peel the layers of fear and constraints, and bring an honest mirror in front of every aspirational leader (gender agnostic)—you won't be able to put it down. This book is an asset for every professional who aspires to grow and may not have the privilege of a coach. Real-life examples, probing coaching questions and a bouquet of best practices will empower every single reader.

Sheenam Ohrie, *Vice President, Dell Technologies*

This book is a reference book for every leader—woman or man—who wants to develop as a leader. It gives you a deep understanding of the factors that make you an effective leader. It gives you a toolkit to understand and peel away layers of your biases, opinions, judgements and your own inner voice that stands in the way of developing as a leader. The unique feature of this book is the set of practices that help you to reflect and develop in your personal journey of leadership.

To get the most out of the book, you need to have the discipline to practice the methods. Try them. They work!

Jeby Cherian, *Chairman, Blubirch, Former Managing Partner, IBM Global Business Services, India/South Asia*

Sailaja has written an inspiring, practical book that will enable women leaders to expand their leadership impact. She has laid out several powerful distinctions that most leaders have perhaps never seen or practised. She has presented these ideas with passion and a strong commitment to building women leaders. I strongly recommend that existing and aspiring women leaders engage in the practices in this book.

Sameer Dua, *Founder, Institute for Generative Leadership, Asia and on Thinkers50 Radar of top 30 emerging thinkers*

What a labour of love and delivery of magic! Sai is that rare blend of a sincere seeker who has done the hard work of her own inner transformation, and is a top-notch psychotherapist and transactional analysis expert as well as a highly experienced leadership coach. Her practice wisdom draws from real-world cases transforming the lives and leadership of hundreds of Indian women; and this much-awaited book arrives just as women in India and around the world are ready to STEP UP to become the 'game changers' they are called to be at this pivotal time. I will be sharing this oh-so-sensible and precious guide for the journey, widely.

Nilima Bhat, *Co-author,* Shakti Leadership *and* My Cancer Is Me, *and Founder, The Shakti Fellowship*

As a Managing Director and CEO, I do see that in businesses within India as well as globally we still face a great challenge regarding diversity. Especially when it comes to females in decisive management positions, the gap becomes even bigger. This book will definitely provide women some special and very interesting additional views and aspects on their way to possibly perform much better in the future. How much it will finally lead to the desired success at the end then still depends on the respective application which is unique for each person.

Klaus Trescher, *Managing Director and CEO, Siemens Technology and Services Pvt. Ltd*

The psychology and leadership blend of the book takes care of the professional and emotional quotient of women. The 'inner work' approach is important to inspire and support more women into being effective leaders. The book will surely guide several women and organizations to create impactful women leaders ... it's what our world needs.

Geetha Kannan, *Managing Director, AnitaB.org India*

Step Up is propulsive, challenging you to commune with multiple dimensions of your inner being—body configuration and sensations, emotions, inner messaging, practice and the store house of historical experiences that sculpt you. *Step Up* is transformational, challenging you to dismantle your inner barriers and emerge from the margins to the centre to be the change you want to see. *Step Up* especially challenges women to interrogate stunting gender stereotypes towards exercising voice, agency, creative power and leadership. *Step Up* draws its 'pulsating with life, change-maker, easy-to-identify-with' trademark from the lived realities of its author—a practicing psychotherapist—and her coachees, brought alive through personal narratives and soul-searching tools. The book grasps you—a must-read for anyone seeking to make a difference, anywhere, at any scale.

(This view is personal and does not necessarily reflect that of UN Women or the United Nations.)

Jean DÇunha, *Senior Global Advisor on International Migration, UN Women; Former Head, UN Women, Myanmar; Former Regional Director, UNIFEM East and Southeast Asia*

Step Up uncovers real challenges that women face while navigating their careers through easy-to-relate examples from Sai's years of coaching experience, and offers an insightful practice-oriented approach towards a powerful transformational experience. This book is a must have for any woman who wishes to unleash her unique self and be an impactful leader in her world.

Shikha Pillai, *Head Strategy*
Siemens Healthineers Development Center India

Step Up is a powerful book and an essential read for women who are ready to design their future and reach their fullest potential. Sai beautifully weaves experiential stories with practical strategies to guide women to enhance their awareness of self-limiting barriers and beliefs, and break through to create a more expansive mindset. This book provides insightful, clear strategies and practices to expand leadership capabilities, skill and presence, empowering women to find their voice and step into their power and potential.

Amy Vodarek, *Executive Coach; Author,* Good Enough: Embrace Who You Are. Unleash Your Brilliance

The content of this book will resonate with most women leaders and emerging leaders too. It really resonates with me. It is simple and yet so powerful ... it empowers. So well thought out and a must-read for everyone who is wanting to make a difference in their live, to shift 'the lens', break the glass ceiling and forge ahead.

Radhika Baliga, *Director—Finance,*
IT & Operations, Jungheinrich

Self-discovery is never easy—*Step Up* enables you to pause, reflect and absorb what you need. You can always come back for more or pick up where you left off with a high degree of continuity and connectedness. What makes this book more appealing is that it spans generations, so no matter where you are in life's journey, there is something in it for you. Most interestingly, and refreshingly (I must say), I found that there is much to learn from the examples of the 'younger you', the 'you today' or the 'future you' across this book. It is most likely to be your 'pick-me-up' book for a long time.

Amrita Madiah, *Director Talent Development, Diversity Champion and Adobe & Women Network Lead, Adobe India*

Sailaja has written an essential read for professional women who want to up their game! She has a powerful way of presenting essential wisdom in a useful and practical way. Readers will be emboldened and empowered to generate their best selves, no matter where they are in their career.

Terrie Upshur-Lupberger, *MCC and author, The Big Re-think*

Step Up does something remarkable as one reads through. Using anecdotes, experiences and theory, it compels one to reflect on one's own past, view patterns and see them playing out in the present, build belief that change is possible and, most importantly, help one work through these changes. It is almost like there is someone who is handholding you, step by step to stepping up. It also brings in a unique understanding to gender and how gender norms play out. Excellent read for anyone who is willing to self-reflect and look at a different realm to themselves.

Madhumitha Venkataraman, *Diversity and Inclusion Evangelist, Founder Diversity Dialogues*

Sailaja combines a sense of perspective, a deep and sensitive understanding of what it truly means to lead from within, with and without a framework that allows everyone be inspired and act. This book is a wonderfully fresh and a practical take on what it means to lead in a highly interdependent world.

Step Up provides a wonderful framework for a dialogue for action between our inner seeker and outer solver. Sailaja beautifully combines a rigorous framework with a toolkit that inspires thoughtful, generous and kind actions, all designed to unfurl the genius within all of us.

Bhawani Singh Shekhawat, *CEO, Akshaya Patra Europe*

Corporate India lacks women in leadership roles. Women are falling behind at every level, especially just outside the gilded doors of the C-suite.

Step Up allows women to challenge the unique barriers to their advancement and explore their leadership potential through a distinctive inside-out approach. The tools used are transformational and a great reference for women to Step Up and start leading!

Neha Bagaria, *Founder and CEO, JobsForHer*

Women take on more 'avatars' at any given time! In her quest to excel at all of them, she starts mentally cataloguing which one can sometimes take a backseat.

Her relationship with her career has been a bone of contention; hence she needs a 'Step Up' to bring it to the forefront to take her on her journey of excellence in her career as well.

Shachi Irde, *Chief Consulting Partner & Advisor to Catalyst Inc.*

STEP UP

Forewords by
Kiran Mazumdar-Shaw and Bob Dunham

STEP UP

SAILAJA
MANACHA

Women's Journey to
IDENTITY, SUCCESS AND POWER

SSAGE

Los Angeles I London I New Delhi
Singapore I Washington DC I Melbourne

First published in 2020 by

SAGE Publications India Pvt Ltd
B1/I-1 Mohan Cooperative Industrial Area
Mathura Road, New Delhi 110 044, India
www.sagepub.in

SAGE Publications Inc
2455 Teller Road
Thousand Oaks, California 91320, USA

SAGE Publications Ltd
1 Oliver's Yard, 55 City Road
London EC1Y 1SP, United Kingdom

SAGE Publications Asia-Pacific Pte Ltd
18 Cross Street #10-10/11/12
China Square Central
Singapore 048423

Published by Vivek Mehra for SAGE Publications India Pvt Ltd. Typeset in 11/14 pt Adobe Caslon Pro by Fidus Design Pvt Ltd, Chandigarh.

Library of Congress Cataloging-in-Publication Data Available

ISBN: 978-93-532-8716-0 (PB)

SAGE Team: Neha Pal, Sandhya Gola, Mahira Chadha and Anupama Krishnan

Dedicated to my daughters—Reva and Zara,
and other young women.
May you walk tall.
May you know your power and use it well.

Thank you for choosing a SAGE product!
If you have any comment, observation or feedback,
I would like to personally hear from you.

Please write to me at **contactceo@sagepub.in**

Vivek Mehra, Managing Director and CEO, SAGE India.

Bulk Sales

SAGE India offers special discounts
for purchase of books in bulk.
We also make available special imprints
and excerpts from our books on demand.

For orders and enquiries, write to us at

Marketing Department
SAGE Publications India Pvt Ltd
B1/I-1, Mohan Cooperative Industrial Area
Mathura Road, Post Bag 7
New Delhi 110044, India

E-mail us at **marketing@sagepub.in**

Subscribe to our mailing list
Write to **marketing@sagepub.in**

This book is also available as an e-book.

Contents

Foreword

India is home to nearly 18 per cent of the world's population, and women make up almost half of that number. We have had pioneers who have broken gender barriers and made their mark in the fields of politics, arts, science, law and business. Many women are today successfully pursuing unconventional professions, as fighter pilots, firefighters, racing car drivers, missile scientists and train drivers.

Several women have demonstrated their business acumen and emphatically broken the glass ceiling in corporate India. We have an undeniable body of evidence to show that companies with greater gender diversity not only do well financially but are also character-ized by better leadership, accountability, innovation, operational efficiency and a motivational work culture. Fortunately, organiza-tions are beginning to see the value that women in leadership roles bring with them. Corporate board rooms are witnessing a higher representation of women, which reflects a changing mindset and affirmative action to channelize the power of women. There has been a steady rise in women in leadership roles from 14 per cent in 2014 to 20 per cent in 2018 across different sectors in India, according to a Grant Thornton report on women in business.

There has also been a steep rise in women entrepreneurs in recent years. India's booming start-up ecosystem is benefiting from the energy of dynamic women entrepreneurs. Of the 6,300 start-ups recognized by Startup India, currently, nearly 2,500 have a woman as founder, director or partner.

Urban Indian society is also increasingly accepting women in this new avatar. It now understands and acknowledges the value of working women in improving the family's quality of life. The soci-etal ecosystem has become more conducive to working women than what it was about 30 years ago. The double income in households has brought in prosperity for the family which has triggered an overall societal mindset change. A pan-India survey conducted in January 2019 revealed that the majority (75%) of men and women in urban India supported women working outside their homes. Similarly, there was overwhelming support (90%) for men and women being paid equally for the same work.

The urban Indian woman has disrupted the status quo of gender roles. Today she is highly educated, professionally competent, independent, career focused, and often, the primary breadwinner in the household. Even though we have enormously talented women professionals in our country, not many of them make a serious attempt at executive level positions at the summit of the corporate ladder. Many tend to give up the uphill task of defying conventions, balancing work and family, and ultimately following their passion of leading from the front.

When I started Biocon in 1978, I faced credibility challenges related to my youth, gender and unfamiliar business model. No bank wanted to lend to me, no professional wanted to work for me and it was a challenge to set up a business because women then were considered as 'high risk' in the business world. I had to strive to establish my credibility as a 25-year-old woman entrepreneur fuelled more by drive and vision than by business experience. However, it was this very drive and vision that helped me set up my business and grow Biocon into what it is today—a globally recognized biopharmaceuticals organization that has put India on the world biotechnology map. In fact, Biocon was one of the first companies in India to appoint women in leadership roles across functions such as quality, human resources and regulatory affairs and so on. These women not only shone in their roles but also contributed majorly to the success of Biocon.

Fortunately, the ecosystem today is more favourable; while the challenges remain, the complexity of these challenges has come down. From my own experience, I can say that overcoming each obstacle spurs one ahead towards new heights of success.

In her book *Step Up—Women's Journey to Identity, Success and Power*, Sailaja Manacha tackles the psychological aspects that women need to address to move beyond the internal barriers that hold them back from leading.

Sailaja says women need to self-reflect and cultivate their inner capabilities to take on leadership challenges and become transformational leaders.

A high level of self-awareness is vital for any leader, male or female, as it boosts one's self-confidence and enables the person to take decisive action, according to Sailaja.

As a psychologist, psychotherapist and leadership coach, Sailaja is able to go beyond theoretical concepts and present practical ideas to create new shifts in the behaviour of women leaders.

As she herself puts it, this book is about learning to say 'I can and I will' in many areas of women's lives.

While I agree it is imperative for businesses and research organizations to change their policies and practices to usher in diversity, I believe women too need to have a strong sense of self-belief and a never-say-die spirit to make it to the top.

As Facebook COO Sheryl Sandberg writes in her bestselling book *Lean In*, 'We hold ourselves back in ways both big and small, by lacking self-confidence, by not raising our hands, and by pulling back when we should be leaning in'.

Across many countries, women have been found to report lower self-esteem than men. Women often underestimate their true value, and this stops them from speaking up in meetings, asking for a raise or seeking promotions.

At a time when women are increasingly being sought out and encouraged to assume leadership positions in many walks of life, from business to community organizations to politics, this book is a timely addition to the reading lists of professional women who are already leaders or are aspiring to accelerate their leadership impact.

In my view, being a woman provides us with special attributes such as compassion, sensitivity, multi-tasking and, above all, the inner strength to excel. With the right mix of skill, experience and resourcefulness, being at the helm can be one of the most rewarding experiences.

As more women take on leadership roles, it will potentially unleash transformational societal change in India that will lead to sustainable economic development, thus ensuring that the fruits of economic development are enjoyed by all. Last year, International Monetary Fund Chief Christine Lagarde had said research showed that raising women's participation in the workforce to the level of men can boost the Indian economy by 27 per cent.

I believe Sailaja's book will be helpful for women professionals, irrespective of whether they are in the junior, middle management or senior levels. I sincerely hope that it will inspire many women professionals to come forward and 'Step Up' to make a mark as leaders in their respective professions in the journey of achieving a fulfilling career.

Today, the entire planet is watching India with great anticipation and you have a world of opportunities before you. Leverage these opportunities and go beyond yourself to help re-engineer the lives of those around you through your leadership, enthusiasm, hard work and the courage of your conviction.

Kiran Mazumdar-Shaw
Chairperson and Managing Director, Biocon

Foreword

There are those of us who face the challenges of our lives with diligent action. Some just manage to face each day to get through it. Some bring ambition to achieve through developing themselves. And there are some who look at the world and imagine what it could be, then make it part of their work and life path to see if they can help the world evolve to a better place.

Sailaja is one of those who have chosen the latter path of helping the world move in a more positive direction by helping many find new paths to the future. We met online from a referral of a mutual friend in 2010 and Sai shared her interest to bring ontological coaching to India. She saw that it was new and rare in India, and held a major promise of helping women in their life and professional paths.

As a psychotherapist, Sai was already in a helping profession and she was already accustomed to bringing the power of vision and big questions to see what is possible. She is an explorer, inventor and developer of concrete paths of practice to enable people to grow themselves into their positive potentials. As a result, she entered our Coaching Excellence in Organizations (CEO) programme and kept her engagement even while navigating large challenges in her own life.

Sai proceeded to integrate her learning of generative principles with her psychotherapy lens and developed her own way of working with groups and individuals through coaching. In preparing for certifying to become a teaching and supervising transactional analyst (TSTA) in psychotherapy, her efforts led her to crystallizing her identity as an innovative teacher with a clear philosophy for impacting change as well as a supervisor of other transactional analysis practitioners.

One of the foundational questions for our generative tradition is 'What do you care about?' We have found that care is the fundamental place in human life from where value, satisfaction and meaning arise. A challenge of our era is that this is a blind spot in current culture and most people live with a level of disconnection from what they care about. Yet finding our deepest cares is a core function of who we become in our lives and what kind of life we live.

In exploring the question of her care, Sai found that, as a woman, the prevalent breakdown of participation of women in leadership roles in our society today is something that she and many others care about. This has led her to her work that is expressed in *Step Up*, the possibility for women to forge a new relationship with power and femininity, and impact the world.

One of our most important blind spots in the world today is blindness to what it is to be human. Our culture has led us to learn, grow up, and encounter ourselves and our world as fixed drifts that we have to navigate within. Yet in her learning Sai has found our generative awareness that human beings are creatures of care and choice, and we can create futures that are not just repetitions of the past. We can be history makers, both in our individual lives and our shared spaces of action.

In taking on women in leadership as a domain of her own leadership, Sai is opening the context for a new perspective, new practices and new possibilities for both women and the world. To change our path to the future, we need to see with new perspectives, open new dimensions of action, and illuminate a path of learning and development that grows us as individuals and enables us to engage with the world as we find it.

In *Step Up*, Sai draws on the foundations of the tradition of generative leadership, which is important because the foundations of generative leadership are based on what is fundamental to any human being. Everyone has a body, emotions and language, and sees their world and acts in it. Everyone interacts with others. Everyone has an impact on others and is impacted by them. Sai has used the generative tradition to empower women in leadership with a focus on action, not just concepts; embody skill, not just understanding; integrate action skills into our whole life journey; and produce real results in the world.

It is by drawing on these foundations of action, interaction and power that Sai has constructed a new path for also dealing with the different challenges that women face in learning and interacting, and in the challenges given to them by their cultures. But the responses of choice, self-development and self-awareness draw from the very roots of our capacities of being human.

Step Up is a major step forward to enriching our cultural understanding of leadership and the path that women can take to harness their gifts and power for the world. Sai illuminates a path not of only concept and inspiration, but of concrete practices and skills, grounded in action, embodying learning and effective engagement with oneself and with others.

Step Up is a path of power and a path for unleashing the contributions of women in leadership. As a path of development, it is a path for professionals based on becoming more effective human beings in life, and as such is a gift to women in every walk of life and to our daughters.

The world and its challenges are calling for a new level and class of leadership, a new level of taking care of people and our shared future that is resonant with a core commitment to productive outcomes. This new level of leadership can only be fulfilled with the full involvement and contribution of women in leadership. May you Step Up to fulfil your own full potential and contribution in the world.

Bob Dunham
Founder, Institute for Generative Leadership
Co-author, *The Innovators Way*

Acknowledgements

I begin my acknowledgements from my roots and where I have come from: My parents who shaped my thinking and encouraged me to make bold choices as a woman—both in shaping my life and my work. My mother's pride in who I am and what I do is a blessing and a source of courage. My family encouraged awareness, choice and the significance of being a learner for life. My sister has been a great source of support, care and unconditional love which I deeply cherish.

My husband Noel has held unstinting support for me and my work. He has challenged me to grow into my better self in all aspects of my work and this is a significant cornerstone in our relationship. Having such a partner is a blessing as he remains invested in my aspirations and has given in every way possible to support my dreams. I am blessed that such a male role model has been available for both my daughters. He has been my greatest ally in all that I do.

I bow in deep gratitude to my teacher of transactional analysis, P. K. Saru, for being a role model of a powerful woman and a model for a potent voice and actions. I carry in me Saru's encouragement, wishes and blessings with pride and gratitude.

Much of the learning on ontology and all my generative leadership learning have come from Bob Dunham. Bob has been extraordinarily supportive of my learning journey through both his generosity and his conviction in my work. He has encouraged me to bring the richness and wisdom as a psychotherapist to this space of leadership coaching and transformative work. I am humbled by his and his wife Josephina's care and warmth, and remain ever grateful for the possibilities they have opened up for me to create.

This book has content and practices based on the work of powerful thinkers, teachers and theorists such as Dr Eric Berne, Dorothy Jongeward, Bob and Mary Goulding, Martin Heidegger, John Austin, Dr Fernando Flores, Dr Richard Strozzi, Thich Naht Hahn and Louise Hay. I am a learner who continues to draw from their works as I move forward.

I have to thank Ms Kiran Mazumdar-Shaw, a leading business-women in Asia and the chairperson of Biocon, for graciously accepting to write the foreword for this book. She being such an iconic woman leader, it is my privilege that this book carries her thoughts on women and leadership.

My client organizations Siemens Technology and Services Pvt Ltd, Cerner Healthcare Solutions (I) Pvt Ltd and Yellow Train School have allowed me to use their examples, statistics and experiences which have provided a great validation for the inside-out approach that I have introduced in this book.

There are several colleagues and those in my personal circle who reviewed the book and provided me feedback—I am grateful for your time and your care—Ragini Rao, Chitra Ravi, Divya Amarnath, Maya Jayapal, Noel Almeida, Newell Eaton, Jude Lobo, Amy Vodarek, Santhya Vikram and Rashmi Verma.

Pranathi Sridhar has been my rock of support for over a year with useful conversations, editing, research and above all holding the clarity of purpose for this book. Her support and remarkable listening have allowed me to breathe easy as I reworked and made enhancements to the book. To Swarnavo Dutta I owe the wonderful illustrations that bring a freshness to this book. Many thanks to Madhavan Pallinisamy for his creative juices on the look and feel of the book, to Sameer Dua, a dear friend and colleague for offering his ideas, eyes and ears to innumerable conversations and navigating the book writing process.

I have one other heroine to focus on, the star of this work.

I use the word 'heroine' and 'star' for all the women leaders who have been part of my journey in bringing this work to the world—for sharing and offering their success stories, struggles and aspirations. They have become shining examples for stepping up and being a designer of one's life and leadership. To each of you women leaders, I honour your journey of breaking barriers, creating your space, finding your voice and bringing your vulnerabilities as well as your best selves as a valuable contribution to this world.

Introduction

If you want to mobilize your strengths to realize your potential, this book is for you.

If you want to find your voice and make an impact in your organization, this book is for you.

If you want to find out what brings you alive at work and find your purpose that you wish to dedicate yourself to, this book is for you.

If you want to expand your possibilities and be a force to be noticed, be it by your peers, clients, teams and superiors as well as your industry network, this book is for you.

If you wish to be a leader of influence in your team, organization and any professional community you belong to, this book is for you.

Step Up is a book about new futures and new possibilities and you can be the designer of both. It is a practical guide that keeps self-awareness and choice as the cornerstones for what you need to do to build the life and work that you want.

The book focuses primarily on professional women like you who are already leaders as well as those aspiring to lead and accelerate their leadership impact.

Step Up is not prescribing a certain notion of success for women. The tools and practices in the book are about YOU deciding what stepping up means to you, and how you wish to do it. This is an invitation to be a designer of your personal and professional life.

My work within the corporate world—both under the banner of diversity and inclusion or just women leadership—threw up issues that women like you struggled with and I knew that the existing conventional model of 'training in skills development' needed to be augmented.

According to Catalyst, a non-profit organization working to build workplaces for women, nearly half of Indian women leave the workforce between junior and middle management levels. In 2018, women held only 20 per cent of all senior roles in India. In 2017, women held only 7 per cent of senior management, that is, CEO/managing director roles.[1]

While courses on speaking assertively, how to network better or building one's personal brand did help women, many women leaders were leading 'blind' as they did not understand themselves, their behaviours or intrinsic motivations. As a result of this 'blindness', they struggled with issues and were stuck in a loop of using solutions that didn't work for them.

In my journey facilitating women's groups I met many talented, bright women. They wanted to move ahead in their careers and wanted to dream big, yet they were expressing stuckness. It is as if they were driving with the brakes on! Stuckness—from not being heard in their families, not being able to negotiate agreements with family members for support they required. Many of them worked on professional issues like struggling to work with male colleagues as their voice was not recognized, some struggled with expressing themselves with authoritative people and some with exercising their power as a leader as they felt compelled to be nice to all in their team. Perhaps these sound very familiar to you too.

Many younger women I met didn't even see themselves as leaders as they thought leadership was only about role, title and assigned

---

[1] *Catalyst Accord 2022: Accelerating the advancement of women*, https://www.catalyst.org/solution/catalyst-accord–2022-accelerating-the-advancement-of-women/ (Accessed on 9 May 2019).

power. To them I would say becoming a leader is about leading ourselves and living the life we wish to. It is about learning to say 'I can and I will' in many areas of our lives. It could be about leading a small or big change in an apartment complex, taking a stance on a polluted lake in a neighbourhood, making a choice for ageing parents as much as it is about leading a project for an organization.

I think that without the understanding of our inner make-up, or our foundation, there is no way for women to deal with the self-doubt, overcome fears and move towards our dreams.

Without the foundational understanding of our inner landscape, we would not be in touch with this 'I can and I will' mindset that is so needed to move the needle in our leadership journey. Without this understanding, we cannot lead with strength and power, responding to the leadership challenges presented to us in today's volatile and ambiguous business environments.

The talent head I was speaking to was briefing me about Reena, one of their business directors who were recently promoted. Reena headed a services business in a well-known multinational. The coaching brief is that she needed to build credibility with key stakeholders in India and across regions, be a leader who her team looks up to and develop her leadership presence. We had a few months of work ahead of us.

When I met Reena what struck me was that I was meeting a very confident leader who knew her job and had grown by being an expert. She was invited to lead for her functional competence and operational excellence.

My first meeting with Reena showed me that she was an introvert and a 'private person' in her own words. She was a tad shy and not very easy with a personal conversation which is what our first coaching session was. I tend to go to the personal initially as it is important for me as a coach to make some high level assessments and understand the coachee, and I could see that it was an uncomfortable space for her. I admire that she brought herself to share despite her discomfort.

Being an execution champion she shared: 'I am very task oriented and I know people value me for the expert eye that I bring to a project'. She continued to give me examples of her successes in challenging times, crisis management and many other examples of her leadership where her competence, drive, brilliance and persistence shone through. However, now she was receiving feedback of rubbing people the wrong way, and individuals were highlighting issues that were being seen as aggressive behaviour. Her own manger had moved to a different region and she was promoted to her current role where she now had to lead a team who were all once colleagues and peers to her.

How would she manage to win her team's trust? What was she able to tell me about each of her team members? How will she view them with a new lens of a leader? How was she going to get past the barriers in relationships that were created in the past due to her aggressive stances towards them? How was she going to salvage a situation with an entire team in a different geography who did not even know her well enough and possibly had heard more stories about her through grapevine? How was she going to build a bigger connect with the entire business of 800 people she led?

I knew I was dealing with a good leader when she faced these questions with great deal of involvement and honesty. She knew she had amends to make, new places to step into relationally, and personal comfort zones she may need to challenge.

Reena came from a simple family, god fearing, hard working with middle-class values. Her family emphasized that education and staying on top performance was the best way forward. She did that year after year through schooling, an engineering degree and early work years. She built her reputation by staying on top of her game through technical competence and becoming an expert. Her task orientedness was her strength, till now. Now it was a barrier. Her main comfort was discussing the task, but she could not connect with the person in front of her.

She learnt to execute well, give what others needed as solutions, get out of the way and not talk about herself too much—a great strength before, now a barrier. She seemed almost robotic, impersonal and distant. How was a team going to relate to this impersonal approach? How were younger folk in her business going to connect with her as their leader?

With her expert hat on she found the toughest of holes to plug. She drove people to execute and in speed. All these were great strengths until then, but now a barrier. A team of competent leaders she now led needed to create, design, be inspired by her, trust her capacity to build a mood of ambition and trust her to help them grow.

Relationships, connection and building trust were the key personal challenges in her leading style. Building relationships not for the sake of ease at work, but for the sake of connecting to the talented people in her team, beginning to appreciate them and develop them. For the sake of becoming a leader they can look up to rather than just follow. She needed to connect with her teams for the sake of rebuilding trust and to tell them that she has their best interests at heart.

Reena needed to begin making space in her mind and heart for her people, for their humanness and failings, their dreams and aspirations—I did not dare to say it in my initial coaching meetings but I quietly held this thought in myself.

Reena needed to begin to bring her 'full' self to her leading style—the lady of shining values, a loving involved mother, and a very caring and loyal family person, someone who had a warm lovely smile that people rarely saw. She needed the courage to show herself fully and come into her own way of leading by balancing power and care. She needed to build the body of a leader who met and impacted others with her presence and her capability to connect. This was going to be our work. I was excited and she met my enthusiasm with her commitment and keenness to stretch herself.

As a practicing psychotherapist and having been on a personal transformative journey myself, I was aware that we women need a map that shows us the influences that have shaped who we are, along with a set of practices and tools to navigate any system we are in—be it organizational or family system. In the personal transformation groups I facilitated, I could see women who changed their belief systems, updated their ideas on gender, and their role in family and society while learning skills to navigate

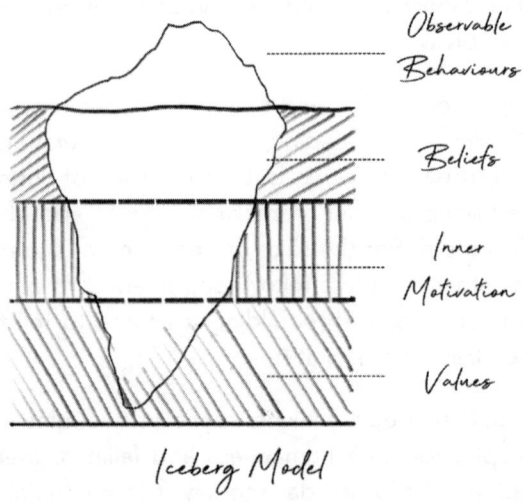

Source: Adapted from Goodman (2002). (1)

tough conversations at home and work. Many of them carried themselves differently, spoke powerfully and appeared like their spine had grown two inches more through the course of these changes. Doing the 'inner work' they did, they began achieving what they hadn't imagined, some began dreaming big and others went ahead and delivered large projects and surprised themselves with their boldness!

So what is this inner work you will need to look into? While much has been said of external barriers for women I think that focus is needed on the 'inner barriers' that have been shaped by family, culture and social norms. Many years of women's exclusion from professional life has had internal effects on us all, as it has shaped what we women believe is possible in our lives. The barriers that culture and family created converted to anxiety and fear to step out, fear to be express ourselves, shine and have aspirations. We learnt to overadapt and overuse our nurturing self in the service of others while disregarding self-care. Our aspirations and our strengths that are ever so relevant in the present day have taken a backseat.

While, collectively, much work is being done at the level of skills and awareness, we need to take a look at the internal workings of what shaped us so that the inner unlearning and new learning can happen.

For Reena, her over drive towards performance, task and her old strategies for success needed examining. The book shares several stories of other women leaders I have coached and the transformations they made.

When I began these transformational programmes, transactional analysis (TA) was the framework I mainly taught and used.

TA is a psychological framework to understand personality, behaviours and long-prevailing life patterns. Hence, it is a potent framework through which we can 'see' ourselves.

Some years ago, I began the Coaching Excellence in Organizations journey with Bob Dunham at the Institute of Generative Leadership, USA (IGL) where I was introduced to ontological coaching and the distinctions of generative leadership.

'Ontology' is the study of being. It seeks to answer the questions 'what makes you who you are? What in the way you see and describe the world creates a unique YOU?' and this fits well with my frame of reference as a psychologist. Fernando Flores is the founder of this discipline. [2] The distinctions I learnt had a new language to explain the human experience to explore our purpose and motivations in life and at work. It also had some potent language for action which I found allowed individuals to action and achieve what they needed to do with others. The learning at IGL also aligned well with my understanding of working with change at multiple levels. Change and transformation work best when we work in all realms of cognitive, behavioural, emotional and somatic.

Taking It to Organizations

I began actively introducing both psychological cognitive frame-works and generative leadership distinctions in my workshops and in coaching. I began creating a hybrid approach that was eclectic as it combined TA as well as mindfulness body practices with gen-erative leadership distinctions. I began weaving in easy-to-access psychological concepts in simple to use language along with some other somatic practices I had learnt on my personal journey.

As women made the inner foundational changes they needed to, they began reporting these shifts in their own behaviours and the organizations started reporting it too!

---

[2] Many of Flores' ideas can be found in Terry Winograd and Fernando Flores' *Understanding Computers and Cognition*, and Charles Spinoza, Fernando Flores and Hubert Dreyfus' *Disclosing New Worlds*.

Some of the changes that the women participants and their organizations saw were:

- Overall increase in confidence and a sense of being 'good-enough'
- Ability to express and speak up more
- Ability to showcase work and be visible in the organization and outside
- Ability to handle 'sticky' and difficult conversations effectively
- Clarity in purpose and motivation
- Ability to feel connected to their real aspirations for life and work
- Capability to see oneself as a leader and lead with care and power in a balanced way
- Greater capability to delegate and lead teams
- Higher capacity to work with tough customers, keep them satisfied and add value
- Greater competence in conversational abilities leading to higher capacity to work with a variety of individuals be it with peers, subordinates or bosses and cross-functional teams
- Confidence to take on high visibility roles in sales, innovation and head design teams
- Higher satisfaction in family life and confidence to face what life throws up

---

Siemens Technologies and Services has over 4,000 employees working in the areas of software research and development, investor relations, corporate finance and audit and functional shared services to Siemens affiliates. GLOW—Global Leadership Organization of Women—is a diversity initiative of Siemens to promote inclusion, networking and inspiring women towards becoming more successful individuals. GLOW in India is a local chapter of the Siemens-wide GLOW network. I have been facilitating the women's leadership programme at Siemens Technology and Services Pvt Ltd Bangalore since 2014.

I had a discussion with both the GLOW team and the participants of the programme to review our work in the past years. The insights I gained from this discussion helped me get a look at how the leadership tools of the book have benefited the women and served the organizations that chose to take the 'inside-out' approach to developing women leaders and continue to do so today.

Shikha Pillai, former deputy general manager at Siemens Technology and Services and a core member of GLOW, shared that women employees constituted almost 28–30 per cent of the workforce. Senior leadership identified that most of the women were at the bottom of the pyramid and not many of them were rising to the top. This led them to enquire into why this was the case. 'We considered the possibility of barriers—not necessarily organizational, but personal barriers such as lack of skills in forming connections, communicating and being visible. A brief informal survey identified that the women had networking problems, a requirement of forums to network, skill-development programmes etc.' Since then the women leadership programmes have been offered to a select group of women employees each year.

Ravinder Singh and G. S. Rajarajeshwari both senior managers and part of the GLOW organizing committee shared: 'We got positive feedback from immediate supervisors of women who attended the programme. They noticed that their approach has grown more positive. They are much more proactive in taking on challenging tasks than before'.

Many women who attended the meeting with me spoke of the impact on their self-confidence, their capacity to have effective conversations with their managers, capabilities to take on bigger impact goals and being promoted to senior roles. Many of them also shared that they felt stronger and also more capable in the realm of their personal lives which in turn energized their capacity and drive at work.

Cerner Healthcare Solutions Pvt Ltd, Bengaluru, is an American healthcare MNC. Since 2016 the Cerner India Diversity Council adopted this inside-out approach to developing leaders and instituted Women in Leadership courses that lasted for three to four months of the year. In the past three years of this approach, they shared that 56 per cent women who had been participants in the programmes were promoted in 2017 fall and 2018 spring cycles. 21 per cent of Women in Leadership participants made it into Drive & Accelerate programme which is Cerner's in-house leadership programme.

Shrinivas Kulkarni, director, associate learning and development, and member of Cerner India Diversity Council, shared: 'The whole diversity and women leadership programmes were new to me. As the head of India operations, I had seen only one woman leader in many years. The statistics show that this programme is a step in the right direction. This year alone (2018), two of the women who participated in the programme were promoted to executive positions'.

Lalitha J. S., senior director and member of Cerner India Diversity Council, shared that she along with the participants managers noted significant changes on a personal level after women employees went through the course. They noticed lesser self-doubt and an increased transparency, along with a clearer identification of their strengths due to which they were able to make strong and impactful decisions.

Taking It to the Streets!

As I continued to work within organizations, I felt discontent as I believed I was impacting too few women. Many women would apply to be at my courses and I would end up meeting about 20! Creating Step Up as an online course was my response to this discomfort. Access to learning, change and growth needs to be in the hands of us women, not just our organization, HR or managers. I wished that more women like you could make the choice to learn and need approvals from no one! Step Up has been running successfully online as a leadership course that any professional woman—either a corporate professional, an educator or an entrepreneur—can be part of. Participants have expressed in every course the value of learning in a community and making big shifts using some of these transformational practices I introduce in this book.

As I developed these new offerings, I remember going through moments of self-doubt myself.

The practices I talk about in this book are precisely the practices that kept me afloat and moving effectively even through those moments of doubt and uncertainty. I love the ambition and energy that the phrase 'taking it to the streets' holds and it captures well my journey of creating Step Up online facilitating women from all walks of life and many parts of India and the world! My dream is to take this learning to girls and women regardless of privilege.

How You Can Use This Book

This is a book born out of my experience of facilitating thousands of women. It is divided into two parts:

The inner self-exploration: It offers you questions and reflections that you will find revealing—what has shaped you? It provides concepts and ideas to link your behaviours, emotional responses and thought processes to what you are seeing yourself do in work and in life. It reveals some typical adaptive patterns women fall into and you may recognize some of those for yourself. I also suggest practices for moving out of these shadows and limiting patterns.

Stepping up tools: They are suggested practices that allow us to move from an internal unexamined personal process to an external actioning of ideas, with self and others. These stepping up tools are actions that allow you to expand your visibility, add value, use your strengths and play big at work. They are in the form of presence practices and the five-finger solution—assessments and assertions, requests, offers, promises and declarations. Practices are central to your stepping up as practices change our way of being!

This book is for a professional woman at any stage in work life! The personal self-reflection questions and the chapters on stepping up tools have been found valuable by most women, be they junior, middle or senior management levels. Professional women returning to work have found the self-exploratory sections very revealing as they often lose a lot of time in self-doubt and inaction.

If you are a leader at middle or senior management level, you may find the concepts on care, presence, adaptive patterns and ideas for change speaking directly to the questions you struggle with. Women leaders have found the practices on presence especially central to developing their sense of calm and confidence in times of leading in a crisis!

I recommend you use this book systematically as it is laid out sequentially, building one idea over another. It will be useful for you to maintain a journal as you read. Journal your responses to the practice questions as well as your insights owing to doing the practices as I am certain you will have many aha moments!

You may find it difficult to keep up with the practices; I suggest you just pick up the ball if you drop it. Be kind to yourself as inner journeys can be both exciting and challenging. Please know that by doing this work you impact not just yourself, but younger colleagues who look up to you, male colleagues who will learn through you and you will impact the next generation you are bringing up!

Reference

1. M. Goodman. *The iceberg model*. Hopkinton, MA: Innovation Associates Organizational Learning, 2002.

UNDERSTANDING OUR INNER WORLD

We all want to be good leaders. We want to lead ourselves, our team at work and our family towards—what we believe is—progress. We want to be able to meet goals that have been set at all these levels. We do realize that to be a successful leader, we require some skills and more. We train hard and learn every skill that the world decides a good leader needs, and constantly stay updated.

But are we missing out on something primarily important?

Our humaneness is the sensitive side of business and often the hidden side too.

We forget about what is happening inside ourselves—our bodies and our minds. We forget that we have to understand ourselves, look within, so that we can begin to change in order to lead ourselves.

Paying attention to our way of 'being' allows us to better understand our external behaviours and inner drives. Way of 'being' can be understood as our 'inner self' and this shapes our 'outer self' or our behaviours.

A leader who loses his voice

I want to share the story of a leader who was successful, loved and respected very much. He was the head of a business unit in a large multinational company. During our coaching sessions, he approached me with a problem that he had been dealing with for a long time. He had some trouble speaking at large gatherings. Whenever he called an all-hands meet, where the entire business unit was attending, he found that he would lose his voice and not be able to address them.

'I know what I have to say. I'm good at what I do. It's not like I have no confidence. I'm absolutely fine in one-to-one meetings and small groups. I don't know what happens to me when I have to speak and make an impact. I don't know what's going on'.

Through our conversations we decided to delve deeper into this problem. We began to understand his 'self'. Unexpectedly, what emerged from these conversations was very intriguing.

He grew up in a small village near Madurai. His father was the headmaster of the local school. In grade 5, this leader was chosen to represent his school at a state-level elocution competition. The competition was in English, not Tamil, which was his mother tongue. To bridge this gap, he was trained extensively. A lot of hopes were pinned on him to succeed because he was from a small village, and he was the headmaster's son.

On the day of the event, he went to the big city fully prepared. When his turn came up, he took his place to begin talking. But suddenly he went totally blank. He forgot what he had to say despite all the preparation. After several anxious moments he finally mustered some energy and spoke whatever he could. Needless to say, he didn't bring any accolades. When he came back, he faced a lot of put-downs, a lot of humiliation. Of course, there was the feeling of personal failure. But there was a much bigger failure that was pointed out to him—that he was the headmaster's son and he had failed. He had failed his father and the village. He had failed all those who expected much from him.

Unknown to him, he had retained that experience within himself. It was surprising how in our conversations this experience popped up out of nowhere. He said, 'I don't know where this has come from. I have not remembered this ever'. But it had emerged in our conversation for a good reason.

Our Personal History Shapes Us

What is the meaning of this experience for this leader I shared about? Every time he stood in front of a large group, suddenly his personal history appeared along with the memory of feeling stuck and frozen on stage. It was all happening unconsciously. It showed up in ways that choked him, blocked him and he would lose his voice each time. In that moment he would forget the successful leader that he is because he was in a different place and time, inside himself.

All of what we experience through our growing years, our years of young adulthood including early years of work—they are all part of the 'self'. This 'self' has memories, full-blown experiences, filled with emotion and vivid images. It has beliefs and ideas about ourselves, the world and situations. All of this forms the 'self' of the leader.

It is not just our thoughts, smart ideas or educational qualifications that we possess. Our profiles on LinkedIn and Facebook or a meticulously composed CV just don't say enough of our 'self'.

We carry our personal history everywhere. We carry it into our homes, relationships and it is present at work each day. We carry it into our meetings and to every interaction and opportunity that we have to present ourselves. Our personal history is present in every moment and affects our behaviours, thoughts and emotional state.

Mathhew Budds in his book *You Are What You Say* explains it potently when he says—'History is the sculptor of our being'. (1)

Our personal history over the years has shaped us. We carry that shape into our everyday experience and we are often unaware of it.

We can see only what we see because we are influenced by our history.

Imagine leading without knowing who we really are! It is like functioning with a degree of blindness and having no connection with what has shaped us.

The 'self' is where one leads from. The question is, what is this 'self'? Is there an entity like the 'self'? What goes into the 'self'?

At the Institute of Generative Leadership USA, I was introduced to a twist in this word 'self' called SELPH. (2) It is a new way of looking at how we show up in situations. It is an acronym for us to acknowledge the different aspects of our human experience.

S: Somatic

What is the somatic aspect in our story? For this leader, it included his experience of being choked. He could do any amount of preparation the previous day, and it would still happen. Inadvertently, the body showed up because the self includes this somatic aspect. The word 'soma' means body.

E: Emotion

The emotional aspect in his case was fear and anxiety. 'What is going to happen when I stand there to address everyone?'

L: Language

We communicate using language, but with language we also create, generate and take action, none of which would come about if we did not speak or did not have access to language. We create out of what we speak as it leads to action in ourselves and others.[1] I bring in another dimension to language, which is the inner chatter and thoughts going on in our mind all the time. In the case of the

[1] I have used the word somatic practices several times in this book. I learnt this from Bob Dunham in the Coaching Excellence in Organizations Programme at the Institute for Generative Leadership, USA. Bob attributes this to Richard Strozzi-Heckler of the Strozzi Institute.

leader it was all that he was saying to himself about the situation: 'Am I prepared enough?' 'When is my voice going to fade?' 'How will this impact what I'm going to say?' Within just a few moments, all these thoughts are rushing through his mind. This dimension of language is about what we converse within ourselves about ourselves and the world.

P: Practices

I interpret this as behaviour that we have come to know very well as we have practiced it for long. His behaviour of becoming tensed and rigid, hesitating to leave his room every time before a public forum and a sense of withdrawing or shying away from that experience—these were the behaviours or practices that he had become familiar with over time.

'I feel like I could really disappear, in that moment', he said during our conversations. His self had practised those behaviours time and again, year after year in his 20 years of work experience.

H: History

We have a personal history. The leader's history showed up unfailingly in how he came across to himself and to others. The failure from the past made itself present the moment he had to speak in front of a large gathering.

Vidusha grew up in a family where her father had a transferable job. Every few years they moved and Vidusha slowly learnt to adjust to new homes, new schools and many new situations. She said, 'Shifting schools and adjusting each time to new forms of studies made me a fast learner and a quick adapter to change'. She found that this quality served her well professionally. Even in campus placements she believed that she got chosen as her risk-taking ability was evident through her responses. She shared, 'I feel anxious but I have got used to going beyond it to function well. I tell myself I know how to manage change'.

June said she grew up in a family where her parents expected a lot from her. She learnt early on to pressurize herself to succeed. 'Now, this pressure has become part of my personality', she said. She pressurized herself to finish fast and in the best way, but forgot to relax and enjoy what she did. Even when it was not required, she set up internal deadlines and pushed herself to give her best always.

It is this SELPH that influences how we exist in the world and acts as lens through which we see and perceive the world. It is as if we are always wearing these glasses, tinted and layered with our SELPH.

The Body as a Place of Learning

I was introduced to the practices of 'somatic coaching' through the Coaching Excellence in Organizations programme in the United States.[2]

Let us take a moment to turn our attention to our bodies and linger on this word 'somatic'.

Our body has an outer physical dimension that is observable. Essentially, this dimension is one of posture and how we hold ourselves. Self-confidence, ease, arrogance, aggression and diffidence

---

[2] See footnote 1.

are all reflected in the muscle and skeletal configuration of our body. Our body also has an inner dimension that is connected with breath, internal musculature and sensations within.

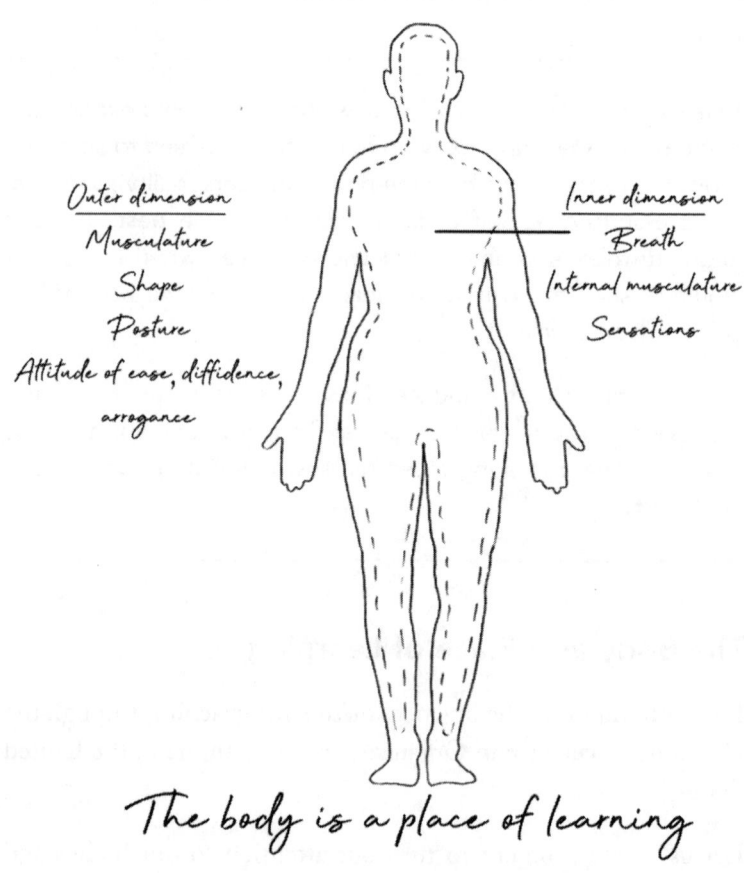

Outer dimension
Musculature
Shape
Posture
Attitude of ease, diffidence,
arrogance

Inner dimension
Breath
Internal musculature
Sensations

The body is a place of learning

Each one of us has a different body from the other; each body moves differently, looks and feels different. Some move with their chest out and a rigid body. Some move with their shoulders stooped and their bodies loose. Some move fast and some slow. Each of us has a shape and I don't just mean tall, short, lean or round. When I say shape, I mean how we hold ourselves and our body, how we sit or stand, our posture, our demeanour and how we move. (3)

As a coach and a psychotherapist, this 'shape' of the body means something to me as it reveals a story of its own. As I work with the somatic dimension, it means something to me when I see people who walk with their waist thrust forward and their shoulders collapsed. It means something when people are rigid when they stand and when they move. It means something when people are easy with their body—they can shift their weight onto either foot and be formal when required, and be really relaxed at other times. Some of us are unaware of how short our breath is and that we never seem to breathe with ease. When some of us speak, our jaws are rigid with barely any movement.

This shape of the body that I speak of is defined by our personal history and our experiences. Therefore, I focus specifically on helping leaders become aware of their bodies during their coaching sessions.

Reena, the leader introduced in the introductory chapter, sat in what I call a 'collapsed' body with a slight hunch. Her voice was nasal and high pitched, and she breathed shallow. She spoke of her current challenges with her direct subordinates, whom she struggled with as she was once their peer, and was recently promoted to a leadership position. I experienced a disconnectedness towards her. I wondered how she may be showing up with her team if she sat in this posture. I also wondered that if I felt disconnected, what may her team experience with her in meetings? When she started a meeting with no greetings but jumped right into problems, how could that task-only mood be for her team?

I decided to check this out. She shared that she felt distant from them and struggled to establish connection. I hadn't yet begun working somatically with Reena, but I wondered what it would be like if she sat up in a more erect posture, allowed her eyes to make more contact and perhaps smile a bit as it could loosen the muscles in her face. I imagined what would happen if this leader just relaxed and breathed easy with an intention of wanting to connect with the person in front of her, not just to know the status of tasks, but to connect to the human being in front of her. She needed to build a body that knows how to connect, listen and be easy. She needed to build a body that came across as both connected and inspiring for her team.

In the workshops I facilitate for women leaders, I am struck by how many women have a 'collapsed' body. Many have a hunch and whether sitting or standing do not hold an erect spine. Their chest is often collapsed which means their lungs are not expanded to full capacity. This impacts how they breathe and how they speak. A large number of them are unable to speak in a loud firm voice. Most have difficulty in making direct eye contact for an extended period of time and have a compelling need to look away or down. Sometimes I have to work consistently over months with these issues as the body had shaped itself in these ways that I see as limiting their leadership. These forms of body language were limiting their impact, voice and expression. Somatic work in leadership is a powerful approach to building the body of confidence and presence, and I have taken much inspiration from the teachings of Richard Strozzi-Heckler and what I have learnt at the IGL conferences.

We notice many a time that there is a certain kind of presence that some people possess. When they are in the room we notice them, when they speak we listen and we don't forget them easily. It doesn't have to do only with how articulate they are or how well they know their subject, but it is also about their somatic presence and their capacity to connect with those around them.

It is very useful for us to become aware—'How do I move?' 'How do I stand?' 'How do I take my space?' Being aware of these aspects including how we breathe is a very useful dimension to developing awareness of ourselves. The space of leadership presence is not just about the mind and our thinking, but also about how we lead by having a certain quality of leadership presence.

The space of trust that the leader builds in an interpersonal context and team context has as much to do with her body as it has to do with what she says. The body is a great place to design 'Who I am going to be and who I will be'. It is a place to notice and bring our awareness to.

Language and Emotion: Listening to Our Inner Chatter

An HR manager that I had coached earlier was the head of her team and needed to make presentations, lead office meetings and speak at all-hands meets. She said to me, 'I am no good at these things…I am a very shy person and am not good when the spotlight is on me… I am an introvert'.

I asked her to describe in detail about how she felt at these meetings.

'I am a nervous wreck and I make it worse by getting tensed from the day before. I can hear it in my head like a constant tape recorder playing—'You will mess up… you are definitely going to mess up'. At events, she became fidgety and kept looking at her notes. She fumbled with her hands even though everything seemed to be going well. She did this in simple presentations as well as challenging ones. She had practised being nervous and fidgety.

I asked her to describe how she handled face-to-face difficult meetings like a tough performance management meeting for instance. 'I begin thinking about the meeting days in advance as I know it is a tough meeting. I find myself saying within that I have not handled such meetings well and am always at a loss of words. The fear of how it will turn out builds up. I work myself up collecting data after data that will help me and rehearsing it multiple times in my head'.

Living in Language

Language is to us humans what water is to fish. The fish do not know that they live in water but they're in it all the time. We as human beings live in language.

Language is used to describe things in the world and it is also used as a way of making meaning of things. It is also that which generates action in ourselves and others.(4) It is also a chatter or a kind of narrative when we're saying in our heads—'This is good, this is not'. 'This is scary'. 'This person is manipulative, I better be careful'.

The leader who lost his voice kept saying to himself—'Oh God, I have to do it again. I hate it when I lose my voice'. This is the language of his inner self. He was unaware of this internal chatter. The 'shy' HR manager was saying to herself again and again, 'I am going to mess up'.

The human mind works in strange ways. It uses language to make stories and narratives of what we see and experience in the world. We make meaning of events, and unknown to us, our mind is spinning and recording a story about them.

The business leader had recorded a story about his incompetence and how scary it was to be in front of a large group. He had promptly forgotten that this story existed. But he was constantly experiencing that story of anxiety and fear every time he had to speak to a large group.

The HR manager had a story that she was shy and an introvert which was why she was not good at public speaking. She also held a belief that she is not good at difficult conversations. Whether it was a simple talk or a complex conversation, she would experience dread and nervousness.

There are hundreds of such stories inside of us. These stories remain in our minds, unaware to us and they limit us in situations where we need to act effectively.

When we are aware of the inner broadcast within us, it allows us to examine it and understand it. It allows us to ask reflective questions, and reveal to ourselves and others what is going on within. In knowing the inner story, we can find ways to weave a new, useful and caring one.

In all these stories, we must acknowledge the space of emotion. Every story carries emotion with it. Emotions shape how we respond to a situation. They shape how we listen. They shape the interactive space that we are in. We are so occupied with content and what we are going to say. We do not ask ourselves—'How am I feeling in this moment?' 'Can I call it out?' 'Can I name it for myself?' We don't have to call it out to the world. The first step is to become aware of it ourselves.

Knowing our emotion is valuable in deciding how to navigate a situation. If not, we will be hostage to our emotions. Emotions are a feedback mechanism because they tell us what is going on within us. Emotions are also very significant as problem-solving tools.

TA, one of the psychology frameworks I use, recognizes four basic emotions—anger, fear, sadness and joy. Most human experiences are seen as permutations combinations of these emotions.

In the case of this HR manager, her anxiety and fear was blocking her. She knew it as 'a dull feeling in the pit of her stomach', but she never actually called it out to herself. When she called it out in coaching, it became evident to her that she could do something about it. I asked her a few questions that helped. What could be the reason behind the fear? Is it true that she 'always' messes up? Were there meetings that went well and she felt confident? What did she do well in those conversations? How else can she prepare besides what she did now? Was there someone who could support her in the meeting? Was there a colleague or friend with whom she could rehearse? All of a sudden she could explore many options not available to her.

I have seen powerful leaders having good emotional awareness and emotional expression too. They feel no hesitation in stating how they feel. I believe that our awareness of our inner chatter and emotions makes us both human and vulnerable. Acknowledging it helps us ease up and support ourselves better. Once we acknowledge our emotions we can find ways to express it or support ourselves so that we do it in a manner that is dignified and effective.

Practice 1

Body awareness

Begin noticing and registering your bodily responses to these situations below:

- What happens to your body in these situations—during conflict, a difficult conversation, when you are with friends you like? Is there a difference in your body's experience?

- When you are with a person who you see as authority, what is your body like? What is your voice like?

- How do you sit or stand while conversing with someone who is distant or disconnected?

- How is your body posture in meetings where you are disinterested in the agenda?

- In meetings do you wait to include yourself in the conversation and what is your body experiencing as you wait?

- What posture do you adopt when someone attacks you verbally?

- How will you describe your voice when you present in front of others?

- How do you breathe when you are upset?

By becoming aware of these aspects, we can find changes in the way we attend meetings or how we communicate. Awareness is the first step.

We can also learn to develop and shape our body to be more effective through many somatic practices we can immerse ourselves in.

Practice 2

Be curious and experiment.

From insights you have from practice, I try these ideas to see their impact on communication.

- Stand with your shoulders pulled back and be aware of your posture in meetings and presentations.

- In meetings, get your feet flat on the ground and your spine erect. Breathe easy and take a moment to focus on what the meeting is about before you begin speaking.

- Experiment with the pace of your speaking and see the impact it has.

Practice 3

Noticing body and emotions

Sit in a comfortable posture. You are going to remember a few experiences as listed below. Do not pick serious or very significant events for these.

Keep your eyes open as you reflect and notice. Notice and label the emotion and note any sensations felt in your body.

Notice if the body feels heavy, light, tight, constricted or rigid. Notice if your breath changes.

This is a good way to connect body and emotions.

- A situation where you were angry with another person. You were a bit upset with them. What were you thinking? As you go over the situation, become aware of your breath and where in your body you feel anger, irritation, annoyance, or if you feel upset?

- Think of an instance where you were a little anxious. Go over the incident and the happenings around it and notice any sensations in your body.

- Has there been a recent event in time when you felt disappointed and sad. Again notice as you go over it and think through the details—what you feel in your body and where. Notice if your breath changed as you recollected the experience.

- Pick a joyous occasion where you felt happy and joyful. Notice the feeling in your body.

References

1. Budd Matthew and Rothstein Larry. *You are what you say*. New York, NY: Three Rivers Press, 2000.

2. Newfield Network speak of an observer being the coherence of B-E-L which is Body, Emotion, Language. Bob Dunham the founder of the Institute for Generative Leadership expanded the BEL model to BELPH where 'P' stood for Practice and 'H' stood for History. He then reframed this from BELPH to SELPH. He has also referred to this in his paper 'The Generative Foundations of Action in Organizations: Speaking and Listening' published in the International Journal of Coaching in Organizations, 2009.

3. Strozzi-Heckler Richard. *The leadership dojo: Build your foundation as an exemplary leader*. Berkeley, CA: Frog Books, 2007.

4. Brothers Chalmers. *Language and the pursuit of happiness*. Naples, FL: New Possibilities Press Florida, 2005.

WE SEE THINGS AS WE ARE

The Observer Is the Hidden Lens

Our early experiences influence our way of being, and this way of being includes how we perceive the world. How the world is for us at any given time, is how we observe things and how we observe is influenced by SELPH.

Once, my colleague and I were attending a meeting at a client's office. The CEO and his leadership team were involved in a discussion. Both of us sat observing quietly. One of the business heads was making a passionate argument about a point while her colleagues looked on—some with attention, others with disagreement on their faces. She continued to speak and the reactions clearly did not deter her. The mood of this meeting seemed tense. It went on in this manner for over 30 minutes.

My colleague quietly whispered—'Wow, that is one aggressive woman'. I looked back at him saying—'I think that is one passionately involved leader—she seems to be driving her point home from a place of deep conviction'. I caught the surprise in my colleague's eyes as I said that.

My colleague and I are different observers of this story. Wonder why?

Our observer is informed by our history and our life experiences—what each of us has experienced, attitudes in our family of origin, places that we've gone to, news items that we have read and the relationships we have been in. All life experiences and the meaning we have made of those inform our observer. At any given time, our observer is influenced by the interplay between body, emotions and language.[1] Our observer manifests in what we say and how we behave.

We Don't See Things as They Are, We See Them as We Are—Anaïs Nin

---

To observe is to make meaning of a situation. As we make meaning, we interpret and reach a personal understanding of a situation. We conduct ourselves based on these interpretations and all are behaviours are guided by this. The observer we are is part of the basic language of ontological coaching that Fernando Flores also used.

Looking through her window

'These people don't know how to wash their clothes. Despite being washed, the clothes don't look clean at all. Either they don't have a good machine or they don't have a good person

[1] I heard this from Bob Dunham in the Coaching Excellence in Organizations programme at the Institute for Generative Leadership USA. I understand that the notion of *The Observer* is central to Humberto Maturana's work in the biology of cognition.

who can wash their clothes', said this woman, who often looked out the window in her kitchen. From this window the neighbour's balcony was visible where they hung out their clothes.

One time, this woman was going out of town. She assigned work to the house help—which was to be completed in her absence. She said to her house help, 'On regular days you can't do a lot of the cleaning work that I would like done. While I am gone, don't do the regular chores, do all of the unusual cleaning work that you otherwise don't get to do'. She left for her vacation and the house help did a lot of work including cleaning and scrubbing many parts of the home.

The lady of the house returned and as usual was working in her kitchen the next day. She looked through the window and saw that the neighbour's clothes were so wonderfully clean. She exclaimed with surprise, 'Gosh at last these people have finally understood. Maybe they got a new machine or they've got someone new who's doing their work well. It is so good to see white clothes that look white!'

Her daughter then remarked, 'Oh you know mum, it looks like our maid has also washed all the doors and windows with soap and water really well. Our windows look squeaky clean, and we can now see clearly through them!'

The change was in the window that she had been looking through all along! Due to the change in her window, her perception of the neighbour's clothes also changed.

She was a certain kind of observer of the neighbour's washing, and how things need to be done. She was a certain observer of herself and how good she was at her own work. There is an observer who is looking at the self and the other.

The observer that we are is a particular kind of lens, and through that lens the world and people look a certain way. This lens, like the woman's window, has some layers to it. Those layers are made of different ingredients that are informing it. One layer is culture, another is personal beliefs, another could be beliefs from our family system, another could be our concept of gender and a layer influenced by what popular media feeds us these days. All these layers are also held within the context of body, emotion and language.

Culture
Family Beliefs
Social Norms
Personal Experiences
Gender Role
Media

The observer has many layers to it

In any situation we are observers who are assessing ourselves, others and the context. From the observer that we are, we act. From those actions, I will generate some results. We act and react from how we observe objects, situations and people. The observer–action–results model was initially developed by Chris Argyris and Robert Putnam. I was introduced to it in the workshops by the Institute of Generative Leadership.

The SELPH is part of the observer and informs it. Our way of being is the way we observe and it is the result of life-long learnings and experiences which remain invisible to us.

The observer that the business unit head from Chapter 1 was— 'I'm not capable, I can't manage large groups. Big groups unnerve me'. From that observer came a set of actions and a set of results that he generated, along with not being comfortable about his body responses and his emotions.

The observer my colleague was in the above example could be: 'Women who speak in this persuasive manner are aggressive'. The observer I was: 'People who speak with this kind of energy are passionately convinced of what they are saying'.

Each of us brings a unique observer into a situation. For the most part, we remain unaware of this observer. It operates beneath the surface of our daily existence, yet it shapes how we view situations, small or big. It is this observer that we are which prompts us to engage in the world the way we do, prompts us to say and do what we do or don't do.

Alan Sieler in *Coaching to the Human Soul* explains how change occurs when there are shifts in the observer that we are, 'When this occurs, a different world is observed and new possibilities for action become available'. These shifts will be in the dimensions of body, emotions, language and as a result in practices too. He goes on to say, 'How we are observing determines what we see as problems, what we see as possibilities and what we see as solutions'. (1) We can see why this can be so powerful, not just in personal transformation, but also for organizational transformation and innovation.

Shaping the New Observer

As a coach my job is to shift the observer of a leader. My invitation is for them to try on a different lens and suddenly what they see changes! Much like what happens when we are at the ophthalmologist. As the doctor changes our lens, we are suddenly able to see clearly. This also means that the lens for each person is different, since the 'eyes' or the observer that each of us are, is different.

With that new lens of observing, we can act differently, thus generating new and more powerful results. Creating a new observer is an interesting place of design for the self.

We can only change what we notice.

Shifting the observer

Another leader who I coached was getting feedback that sounded like this—'You're very defensive as a person. You're not easy to work with'. 'Some people find you really sticky'. 'You offend people with your directness'. 'People have to be spectacular in order for you to trust them'.

During the coaching sessions, her observer was revealed to her. She realized that when she was around people whom she thought were being manipulative, or whom she assumed were not being completely transparent, she labelled them as dishonest. Each time they misinterpreted information, she saw them as slimy. From the observer that she is, came a set of actions.

She became cautious and guarded around these people. She asked them more questions than she would ask other team members. She withdrew from this set of 'slimy' people and established a very transactional communication with them. In her mind she was saying—'I don't want to do too much with these set of people who are "dishonest"'.

This was at the root of how people experienced her and the feedback that she received.

When she became aware of the observer that she was, it opened up a new possibility for her. She saw the SELPH pattern that had roots in her personal history and family origin. She grew up in a family that had relatives who took advantage of her mother and grandmother. Caution and suspecting people's intentions were an integral part of her observer.

Once she noticed her observer, she was able to join the dots in several situations where she used this 'overcautious' observer. The new observer noticed her inner thoughts and emotions and began regulating her reactions. She learnt to question her judgemental labelling of people. She decided that she needed to sharpen her skills of clarification. Her new observer decided that respect was going to be an important part of her leading style.

She began to pick up skills to ask questions from a place of enquiry instead of inquiry.

She started building a connection with people in a non-defensive and easy manner. The next appraisal feedback had a turn-around effect. The rumblings in her team settled and she felt happy about her capability to build a connected and open team.

She even began smiling more at those she met. In about 6 months, she felt that she had become easier with the people around her.

In the above story, the manager developed a new observer. This observer was more trusting of the world. From this new observer came a new set of actions that she began practising. Within few months of practising the new actions, the level of trust and comfort in the team grew. She began to see new results that she hadn't seen before.

Once we have new actions and results, these are again reflected on and integrated into the new observer we are and this learning cycle goes on.

> The range of what we think and do
> is limited by what we fail to notice.
> And because we fail to notice
> there is little we can do
> to change
> until we notice
> how failing to notice
> shapes our thoughts and deeds.
> —RD Laing

New power for self

In a recent workshop with a few emerging women leaders, I worked with Suchitra. Suchitra had some new ideas of what she wished to do to establish her identity in her team, and many of these ideas were connected with technical competence and upgrading herself in this area. The observer she was sounded like this, 'Sai, I am very poor in this area as I have neglected it for many years now'. 'Even if I begin, it is going to be such an uphill task'. 'What if I show up as incompetent and lacking? That would be so embarrassing'. Her body seemed collapsed and emotionally she was overwhelmed with the anxiety of making the effort.

The observer that she was held herself to a very high standard. Her observer possibly held ideas of perfection, looking good in front of others, failure as embarrassment and that as a manager she needed to know everything really well. I knew that it was a tall order and each one was worthy of examining. As I coached her, she began noticing the observer that she was. She realized that she cannot know everything and that as she journeyed, she would make mistakes and learn through it. She shared that she came from a home where perfection was encouraged and any lesser standard invited criticism or worse—punishment. Her observer had unhelpful ideas on how to be a good learner.

As we spoke, she continued to build on these new ideas and her body became relaxed and her shoulders dropped. Her face relaxed into a smile. She began to notice how her observer limited her capacity for positive action. She noticed that her observer was stuck in an old story that was not helping her learn. I could see she was breathing easier now.

She decided to update her observer. 'I can be a dignified beginner'. 'I can ask for support as I learn'. 'I will learn by doing'. 'I will aspire for excellence not perfection'.

In a few months, this manager had made a clear plan on how to upskill and had even announced to significant others about her plan to present on some technical areas. She joyfully reported that she constantly reminds herself that she is a 'dignified beginner'.

Suchitra's story is a great example of shifting the observer for new actions and new results.

The next time we are in a challenging situation, if for a moment we stop and examine the observer that we are—we may find that maybe, our lens just needs some cleaning.

Practice 1

Awareness of your observer

Pick a recent situation where you had a minor conflict. Ask yourself:

- What am I thinking about the situation, others and myself? What other layers exist to my lens? Where have those layers come from? By whom are they influenced?

- How are those layers influencing how I act?
- What if I have to apply a new way to look at the situation?
- Do I know someone who might respond differently to this situation?
- How does that change my action? How does it change the way I might behave?
- How I may feel different with the new lens? How could that create a new way of being for me?

In a meeting that you are attending begin to notice and listen to your inner chatter.

If you have the luxury to write down some of that chatter, do it. See what it reveals about the observer you were at the meeting.

Ask yourself what shift would be useful for you? What shift would allow you to be more effective and productive given your role in this meeting?

Reference

1. Sieler Alan. *Coaching to the human soul: Ontological coaching and deep change.* Vol. 1. Australia: Newfield, 2003.

MANY PARTS TO OURSELVES

I was introduced to TA two decades ago. It was a fascinating framework with concepts—both simple and complex. It explained the ups and downs of the human condition, the formation of our personal narratives as well as our relationships in a powerful way. Despite being a student of psychology for years, I had not come across such a lucid explanation of the human personality that was so relatable. I had not seen a framework that articulated so elegantly the connection between our early years' experiences and how they shaped our personality, emotional life and our behaviours. I became a student of TA, then a psychotherapist, and then a teacher and supervisor in TA psychotherapy. It has been a fundamental cornerstone of knowing myself and a framework that guides me in my work as a coach.

TA is a humanistic framework with a theory on personality as well as an explanation of our psychological structure, life narratives and how all of this impacts our communication and relationships. It links beautifully to the observer in us and the SELPH we each have, so we can understand the various stories we hold within us.

Eric Berne, the founder of the psychological framework, TA, made a stellar contribution to understanding human behaviour when he identified three parts that make up our personality. He named these parts the Parent ego state, the Adult ego state and the Child ego state. Berne defined ego states as—'A consistent pattern of feeling and experience directly related to a corresponding consistent pattern of behaviour'. (1)

Parent Ego State — Sometimes we think, feel and behave as our parent figures

Adult Ego State — Sometimes we are rational, resonable and present to the here and now reality

Child Ego State — Sometimes we think, feel and behave like the child we once were

Parent ego state: When we think, feel, behave like a parent figure.

Adult ego state: When we are reasonable and think, feel and choose behaviour relevant to the here and now.

Child ego state: Sometimes we think, feel and act like a young child or person we once were.

The Parent Ego State

I remember spending a lot of time with my cousins at their home, during my summer vacations. My aunt was a strict disciplinarian. All I remember of her were commands and instructions. She had an uptight rigid body and a tough-looking demeanour. I do not remember her ever smiling at me. I was utterly terrified of her almost all the time. I remember something that she often did. Even now when I think of it, I feel a jitter through my body. If she was upset with her daughters, she would call them to the dining table and all she did was give them a scary glare and said 'SAY'— and they would meekly say in chorus, 'SORRY'. She didn't say what she was asking them to say sorry for and they didn't know. They just did it each time—because of the power of a commanding stare and voice, the power of position and authority, and the power of body language.

As I write this, I also remember the wonderful goodies this aunt made when we kids visited and the care she took of our food and play. Yet, these fade into the background and the above image of her tough self prevails in my memory.

Parent ego state in its controlling and commanding form is quite similar to my aunt. The other more popular character that comes to mind is the character of the father in the popular Bollywood film *Dilwale Dulhania Le Jayenge* (DDLJ), played by Amrish Puri. He is the typical angry, authoritative father—one whose word is considered God's word, one who knows it all, and is commanding and condescending.

The Parent ego state shows up in two forms: Controlling and dominating or Nurturing and caring. (2)

If our parents were kind and caring, we are likely modelling to be that way; if they were judging and scolding, we are likely to adopt some of that in our lives.

This is because we as children, while growing up, often unconsciously take other people's personalities into ourselves. The psychological word for this process is 'introject'. We can think of it as 'absorption' of behaviour. When we are young, we are like a sponge. Unknown to us, we are absorbing other people's gestures, expressions, feelings, thinking and worldview. We have copied many aspects from significant parental figures and people we considered as authority in our lives. Apart from parents these could be grandparents, teachers, older siblings, friends and mentors too.

All of the absorbed aspects become part of who we are and are stored in our Parent ego state. As grown-ups, we borrow from this place and may behave like one of them. We may speak and express similar thoughts, and even feel the same feelings as they felt in response to a situation. We may even have the same emotions, attitudes and body language that they held towards different situations. This becomes part of our SELPH.

The Parent ego state has collective messages passed on from generation to generation. This is also what we come to see as cultural messages. Cultural norms fit in the Parent ego state. These messages have directives, instructions, and dos and don'ts.

Some of these messages are also about defining femininity and what a woman's role in life entails. It has messaging around who is a 'good girl' and who is a 'good woman'. These messages are part of the observer we are. Being aware and examining some of these definitions is part of the inner journey we will make as we transform ourselves. Doing this, develops a new observer.

Here are some messages culturally scripted:

She is a good woman, she makes many sacrifices.

She is a good mother, she is always attending to the children's needs first.

Girls should be quiet.

Smart girls can be clever—but never show how intelligent you are. The boys may not like it.

A woman should stay with her husband no matter what.

A lady is never loud.

Teaching jobs are great for women.

What can one expect? She is a woman after all.

While these kinds of messages carve a role of what a woman should be like, if we are unable to fit these descriptions, it creates an anxiety in us.

Parent messages are like tapes in the mind—they keep playing on and on inside our heads. These form consistent language or inner chatter in us. A small trigger is enough to activate these tapes. Some tapes are activated very often and some are situational—certain instances trigger the tapes. The active tapes for some of us maybe are: 'You are not good enough'; 'Be quiet'; 'Stay back—you don't have to be important'. For some of us these messages may show up in specific instances such as in a meeting with significant people or in a performance appraisal discussion, during conflict or when we wish to express our views.

When I began my own transformational journey I met P. K. Saru—my TA teacher. Saru was such an interesting combination of nurture and structure. She had a commanding personality, a powerful voice and a manner of speaking. As a therapist and a teacher, she had a powerful nurturing presence—someone who could read the emotional layers beneath the words. Her questions and conversations would get us thinking and reflecting. She would be very quick to remind us about the power within us, our personal resources and capacity for positive action in our lives. She was a potent role model for each of these actions.

It was refreshing for me to experience a Parent ego state in this form. She was firm, and yet was a powerful manifestation of the nurturing element of the Parent ego state. That part of ourselves that is caring, supportive, encouraging and kind. We absorb these aspects also into ourselves.

Messages from this part of the Parent state create tapes that are helpful and supportive. They keep us feeling cared for and happy. They encourage us to attend to ourselves and to be what we wish. They serve as a storehouse of motivation and positivity, and get us moving in the direction we choose. They help us stay confident and feeling good about ourselves.

Parent Voices in Our Head

Parent voices are voices that may actually be of one of your parental figures. We may actually hear their voice with the same intensity, tone and manner they speak in.

Parent voices play like tapes inside of us

Some of us have heard great messages in our tapes. These become part of the observer we are:
You are smart.
You are intelligent and resourceful.
You can be what you want.
You think well and make clear plans.
Take care of yourself, your health is important.
You are precious.
Some of us have banal messages in our tapes:
You are stupid.

You don't get it.
You are too slow.
You are never going to amount to anything.
Go away! No one asked you for your opinion.
Don't speak, you're not being asked.

Here are a few instances that I have seen women express in groups I worked with, and some of these probably are familiar:

A woman who is being loud and excited at an office party may hear, 'Good girls don't behave loud', and then she clams up. She may feel like dancing and swaying, but the parent voice may be heard as punitive and the inner child responds to it. She becomes conscious of herself and decides to be quiet.

A woman may feel uneasy because the promotion she got will mean that her salary is more than her husband's. The parent voice says—'That is not okay'. She has often heard in her home the saying that 'It is good to be a step behind the husband. After all, he is the breadwinner of the family. His self-esteem should be taken care of. Earning more can be threatening to his self-esteem'. 'Women work so they can keep busy and can balance home and family'. Her main job was to take care of home and kids. When she knows that she will earn more than her spouse, this goes against the parental directive of being a step behind.

A successful woman may discard an option to relocate with a promotion because 'Women should not leave family and travel'. She is worried about upsetting status quo as she is unsure how the family will cope. Her husband is supportive but surely it's not a man's job to follow his wife to a new city isn't it? Again, the parental directive plays out. It is her job to care for the family—she is the heart of the home. How can she be upsetting the apple cart?

A working woman feels guilty when she receives many awards because 'It is not nice to outshine your husband'. She has seen her mother being subservient and passive. Her father was always the key person in the home—the all-important person. Her mother may have been creative and talented, but she kept those to herself. This is part of her Parent ego state and now she has no right to outshine him. How will it appear to him and rest of the family?

Parent Actions Reflect in Us

When we behave in the same manner as one of our parent figures did, we are definitely using behaviours stored in our Parent ego state. (2) I have outlined a few examples here:

When we criticize a colleague we may be doing it in the same manner as one of these 'bigger' people did.

When we scold a friend for not eating on time we may be using the same tone and words that our grandmother may have used.

A girl who sees her mother behaving like someone who is helpless, may decide that it is part of being a woman, and she now behaves helplessly in matters of money.

We may postpone or ask our spouse to make a decision because we always saw our mothers asking our fathers first and not having an opinion of her own.

Updating the Parent Ego State: A New Version

We can think of our Parent ego state as a computer or a machine. Computers need upgrades and maintenance too. At times, they need an additional memory card to hold more information and to increase processing speeds. At times, its entire software needs updating! It is the process of developing a new observer in us, especially from the gender dimension.

We must allow those updates to happen and remove old, outdated beliefs that are not useful anymore, delete old and limiting behaviours that we borrowed, especially the ones that no longer serve us. We must examine and keep the ones we want—those that are uplifting and useful.

The Child Ego State

When a parent voice says: 'You don't get anything quickly do you?', who do you think is listening to that voice? The inner Child in us is often activated with the Parent voice. The inner child responds: 'Yes I better be quiet'. In some of us the inner child adapts and in some of us it may be ticked off and rebel against this voice. All of this happens unconsciously. We carry these patterns of responses into our adult life.

Each of us has a 'little self' within us. In fact, we have many little selves from the different ages we were. Have you seen a cross section of a large tree trunk? It has concentric circles within it. Think of each circle as a specific age. The age of the tree is recorded in this manner. The Child ego state is similar. It holds each age within it. The memories, experiences, thoughts and feelings at each age are all recorded and stored in the Child ego state.

Behaving from the Child ego state does not mean we are being childish or immature. Instead, a better understanding would be to see our behaviour as childlike. It means that even though we are 35 years of age, at times we may behave like we once did when we were young. Since each of us had different experiences as young people, each of our Child ego state is different.

The Child ego state shows up behaviourally in two ways: Adapted or Free child. (2)

The Free child is characterized by high energy, uncensored impulses, affection, curiosity, spontaneity, feistiness and playfulness. Some of our families were accepting of such expressions while others may have stopped us, thereby curbing our spontaneity.

In the way our society is constructed, only some parts of the Free child are accepted in women. Many other parts we are asked to withhold. Women keep those parts hidden and let them out only when they are in environments that accept it.

A client once told me how she was walking through Cubbon Park—a wooded and beautiful park in the middle of Bangalore city. It was a beautiful day and flowers were blooming all around. Bangalore city is resplendent with orange, yellow and lavender from the jacaranda trees. She began swaying the arms of one of her daughters and began singing one of her favourite Hindi songs in a burst of energy. Her daughter was most aghast and embarrassed and asked her to stop immediately! The lady said to me how surprised she was that her 15-year-old daughter had already developed an observer that was not dissimilar to her own parents. It was the same way her parents may have reacted to her swaying her hands and singing

A coachee in one of my discussions felt that most great leaders have a strong presence and visibility. She thought they come across as people who speak confidently and take up challenging tasks. She believed that visibility is directly proportional to leadership. However, she had this idea of herself being 'childlike' at work due to her appearance. It was probably how others perceived her as well. She then took on a new project and presented it to the CEO, and she was finally visible to all as someone who was capable. She always knew that she was capable of handling bigger and more challenging projects and reflected that in her work. She even began to receive more challenging work after her presentation!

Expressiveness is the hallmark of the Free child. Yet girls are often told to curb spontaneous expression.

Don't get dirty
Don't do this, don't do that...
(calm down, curb that curiosity)
Keep quiet.
Do what you are told.
(Curb that tendency to speak up and ask for what you want)

Women get shaped into being more 'overly adapted'. How come?

Remember Simran? The damsel in distress in DDLJ? The poor woman who could not speak up, the good obedient daughter who upholds family honour and obeys every command of her parents? It appeared like she decided not to use her mind or her voice. She passively accepted all that was demanded of her, while continuing to be nice. She was the perfect daughter who does it all.

Yes I will' and 'Sure I can' is a simple way of describing the Adapted Child. She is trained to comply, be nice and adjust. To be saying 'yes', even if we wish to say no is a classic example of the adapted child.

When in the presence of parental figures and those we consider as authority, the Adapted Child may show up just as it always did when it was younger. This part of us is socialized to understand societal norms and expectations. Learning to say 'please' and 'thank you', and to do what people expect of us is a good example. This keeps relationships going easy—we are told. Meeting expectations got us approval, positive strokes and caring from the elder people who laid down these expectations.

As girls, some of these adaptations we were expected to make were not all helpful. Many adaptations are irrational, inappropriate and do not fit the times we live in now. Many are unnecessarily limiting and inhibiting in nature. We have carried these adaptations into our adult life and continue using them. These adaptations are some of the ways women give away power, lose voice and do not show up as leaders.

Some of these adaptations are patterns that we commonly notice in women.

1. I am not smart enough

Many of us adapt by playing down our intelligence. In fact, some of us act confused all the time. This hampers our ability to make independent choices, make decisions as well as impacts our capacity to be successful and ambitious for ourselves.

Many of us are encouraged to trust the judgment of others rather than our own.

Some successful women I know believe that, 'All significant financial decisions need to be made by their spouses'. When we were young many of us were told, 'Parents know best'; 'Elders know best'. The meaning we pick up is, 'Don't rely on my own thinking'. (3)

A coachee shared—'I have seen my father rejecting my mother's ideas all the time. His opinion was all that counted. I don't think much when my boss constantly rejects my ideas. I know I have good ideas, yet I play it down. He may listen to the same idea from another person on the team, but seems closed to mine. I have not allowed it to bother me too much and now I understand why. A woman's thinking being discounted is familiar to me. I have learnt to accept it as part of life and move on. Moving on with acceptance is part of my observer. As a result I do not insist that I am listened to, I do not repeat the point I have made. I do not ever speak with conviction in team meetings'.

Reflection:

Do you see some of these in you and in other women you know? Make a note of what you resonate with.

- Lack of confidence
- Often having to ask others to help
- Not being able to take a decision to end what is harmful for us
- Feeling victimized at work
- Needing continuous feedback from others that they are doing fine
- Feeling inadequate despite being good at work
- Getting deflated and depressed with criticism small or big
- Saying 'How could I have done such a stupid thing?
- Feeling they do not measure up to others

2. I need to be pleasing

Another very common adaptation we are socialized into as girls is to 'be nice'. Most girls are expected to comply while following rules and norms. A boy who is playing loudly and romping about is ok as 'Boys will be boys', but a girl who does the same may be called loud and clumsy. Instead, when she is being polite, smiling, listening and doing what is told she is called 'a good girl'. We internalize this need to please others and begin caring immensely about what others will think of us, our looks, our work, our competence. We are not ourselves. (3) I really like this poem by Dorothy Jongeward (4)

I see myself through the eyes of others.
I hate waking up wondering what they think of me.
Am I ugly? Am I beautiful?
What shapes do I form in the eye of their mind?
Oh, God, hope they like me
Please let them like what they see.

'Taking on more than what we are capable of doing in an effort to please or appease others puts our integrity at risk', say Amy Vodarek and Anne Day in their book *Good Enough*. (5) They suggest letting go of the need to be liked as it is freeing and allows us to be ourselves, making choices that align with our needs.

A course participant shared her performance appraisal experience. She was a manager with over 10 years of work experience. She shared that she was given a good rating by her manager. However, it was not what she was expecting. Given her contribution, she imagined that she would get the topmost rating. She was disappointed and began sharing the data she had about her contributions. Her manager accepted her points only partly and had many comebacks for what she had to say. She then shared that she lost steam in the meeting as she felt she did not have it in her to counter what he was saying. 'When people put up a hard argument, I cannot hold up. I give in because I feel that me speaking so directly and so much will cause unpleasantness and I don't like that. I cannot handle confrontative conversations'.

As a result of this observer in her, she kept quiet. She came away without expressing her disappointment. She went through the year feeling demotivated as the hike in her salary was far from what she had expected.

If there is one pattern that I see the most, it is this adaptation of pleasing and finding it difficult to say what we need to. (2) It is a skill and a practice. Saying what we need to say, doing what we need to do, need to become second nature to us. We need to be more daring in what we want to say.

Reflection:

Do you see some of these in you and in other women you know? Make a note of what you resonate with.

- Yielding to others very quickly
- Not being able to say 'no'
- Not willing to make a complaint if something isn't up to the mark
- Taking bullying from customers
- Not being able to ask for a raise and negotiate
- Not expressing displeasure at a poorly-defined role
- Anxiously moulding herself to others needs
- Not being able to reject poor opinions that others have of her
- Not expressing her opinion lest she upsets somebody
- Bending backwards to accommodate even when she cannot afford it

3. I need to get it right

As young girls we are given messages like 'Whatever you do, do well'. We get approval and strokes when we do perfect jobs. (2) For some of us our early training is not to speak unless we know it well.

A client told me that her pet name at home was Dadima! Imagine a young one being called grandma. That is because whatever she spoke was so thoughtful, wise and perfect. She received lots of positive comments for how smart, intelligent and knowledgeable she was. Parents felt proud they had such a perfect daughter who was good, obedient and to top it all, intelligent enough to make such good conversation. Phew!!

When we do a task well, we may be told that it can be done even better and we may be shown an example of perfection. No matter how much we do and how far we go, we may be shown that there is always another level of superbness possible. Hence, we learn to strive and we don't feel good enough most of the time.

I was coaching Julia—a media person who worked in the field of marketing at a large corporate company. She was also trained as a script writer and filmmaker. While she was quite happy with her work and her role, she had been feeling an itch for a while to go out and make a film by herself. She had a script roughly written out and now had to begin to tap her network to see if there were people keen to fund it. However, she had not made a single move for months together as she felt the script wasn't ready to be shown yet. She wanted to tweak it, perfect it and then put it out. After all it was a reflection of her, so it needed to be perfect! So she said she planned to 'Work on it a little more.'

Another dimension of the 'getting it perfect' pressure is the imposter syndrome. Fear of failing, not meeting expectations others have of us is a constant companion. As a result, we strive hard to show our perfect self and our perfect work externally while being constantly fearful internally. It develops a fear in us that others will know we don't have it all together and that we are phoney.

I have coached many women who put on a false face that is stoic even though they are falling apart internally. Women share that they feel societal pressure to prove their competence and hence they live through the charade. Amy Cuddy speaks about the imposter experience in her book *Presence* as being a 'kind of social anxiety'. (6)

Amy had certain qualms about a new role that she was offered. She shared, 'I am occupying a new position as HR business partner. This position came my way a couple years back as well, but I was not a risk-taker back then and so I decided not to take it up. This time when the role was offered to me, I was looking at it through a different lens. I worked with the mantra that "Sometimes it is okay to take it easy. It's okay if you are not the best all the time and I don't know it all". It got me thinking that if I do take it up, I will take some time but I will do well.

I am now going to take up the new role and I attribute this decision to the programme I went through as it made me more insightful and self-aware'.

Reflection:

Do you see some of these in you and in other women you know? Make a note of what you resonate with.

- Striving, striving, striving
- Feeling what you have done is not good enough
- Needing to labour over things simple or complex
- Belittling yourself often as you hold high standards on any task
- Constant comparing and wondering about others' judgements
- Not being able to delegate work as others will not do it as well
- Not being able to start in the wait for the perfect time
- Overthinking simple things so you get it perfect

4. I can't

We are told that what we have to contribute is no good or we are put down when we show our thoughts and feelings. We learn to be a 'nobody', a 'wallflower' or 'furniture'—we don't really notice wallflowers do we?

We develop passivity patterns. These patterns stop women from showing up where they need to and stops them from effective problem solving. They end up just waiting. (2)

Simran from the Bollywood film DDLJ is a great example of passivity. Waiting for someone to rescue her; waiting for permission; waiting to be told what to do; waiting to do what is important for herself. In fact, most of our film heroines are often shaped with big doses of passivity while the men in their lives are proactive and solving problems. How is that for social reinforcement?

Sunaina was a project lead. She shared that she had many ideas for changing her team environment. She had a special interest in leadership, personal development and human processes. Owing to this, she believed that she had ideas to resolve team communication and issues of teams working differently. She had been wanting to work on a team manifesto and run it as a workshop for her business. However, these were all ideas in her mind. She said that she thought too much and never took action on it. I enquired if she had shared this with her manager and the business head but she hadn't. She stayed with this idea in her head for a whole year. Such a loss for her team, her business and for herself to shape a public identity as a contributor and as someone who adds value beyond her role as a project lead.

Reflection:

Do you see some of these in you and in other women you know? Make a note of what you resonate with.

- Sitting quiet in meetings
- Waiting for their turn to speak even though they have clarity
- Waiting instead of getting on and doing what is needed
- Contributing their thought only when they are invited to
- Not being able to be direct about what they want
- Behaving helplessly
- Waiting for a better day, a better time (which is elusive and never seems to come!)

The four main adaptations in women

The Adult Ego State

Independent thinking, being objective and being centred in awareness is the forte of the Adult ego state.

We use this part of our personality to test current realities, looks at pros and cons of an action, understand the data and information we have access to. It is that part of us which is present to the here and now realities. It also uses all our senses to feed us information that is important to problem solving. (2)

Julia—the script writer coachee is a great example to go back to. There she was with her wonderful ideas on the film and her half-done script but paralyzed with no action whatsoever. The coaching session was about that. As any coach does, questioning and exploration is what I did using my Adult ego state. I needed to do so because Julia was in her Child ego state—anxious and inactive. Some questions we explored were—What does she really care about in her professional life? What truly excited her? Five years ahead, what will she want to look back and feel good about? All of it pointed to making the film.

But she spoke of her self-doubt of not being ready enough and getting her script perfected. She spoke about her doubts and anxieties of how it will be received. She also had self-doubt if she had lost touch with writing as her current marketing role did not give her too much occasion to hone that skill. The demons in her mind were plenty and the battles of 'Should I vs I shouldn't' raged on. The parent voice in her mind told her it is stupid to give up such a good, lucrative career. It is too big a risk in her late 30s as she had other responsibilities.

We then explored the small steps idea. She decided to take small steps that she did not feel threatened by, small steps she could action and small steps that allowed her to 'test the field' before jumping in!

She decided she would write out a concept note. In order to write this, she would need to speak to a colleague who would support her in thinking through it. She would contact just three people in her media network so she can discuss the idea and receive feedback. She also decided she would join a weekend script writing course to deepen her skills and be back in the creative space as it would aid her process of writing again.

By the end of our conversation, she felt relieved and joyful. It is indeed interesting what happens to us when we are in the presence of another who stimulates our Adult ego state. It seemed to me about 30 minutes into the conversation, that the wheels in her mind had got unstuck and begun moving. It appeared like she was questioning the validity of the parental voices and soothing the fears and anxieties of her inner Child. Her observer had shifted and she was beginning to use her Adult ego state energy to generate options for herself that didn't exist before. This is a lovely example of a new observer leading to new actions.

The kind of recognition and strokes a woman is given for her intelligence and independence is directly connected to the quality of how her Adult ego state that develops from a young age.

A woman using her Adult ego state will value self-awareness. She gathers new information, analyses available data and thinks things through. She will test out current realities, ask questions to clarify and will be open to new information that supports her problem solving.

Reflection:

Do you see some of these in you and in other women you know? Make a note of what you resonate with.

- Not making contributions even when they know they can
- Not asking questions
- Taking all that is presented at face value without questioning
- Not looking for information that supports solution finding
- Going with assumptions instead of testing it
- Not clarifying when in doubt
- Being stuck with decision due to not weighing both sides
- Becoming blank or confused in the face of tough situations

What Helps Us Move Out of Our Adaptations?

The Nurturing Parent Ego state turned towards ourselves!

In TA, we call it the internal Nurturing Parent—using the nurturing, caring and encouraging parts of us to serve ourselves. Women are happy to exercise this part outwardly towards others—caring for them, nurturing and supporting their endeavours, being of service and looking after others. It is time to turn this inward.

While coaching a business leader in a medical equipment company I encountered her making harsh judgements on herself. The critical Parent ego state was very active and it seemed to be berating her. She seemed to hold extremely high standards of performance for herself, much higher than what she might hold for others. As a result, she often felt depleted, tired and under tremendous pressure. She did not give herself enough rest and was becoming forgetful because she was overwhelmed. Talking to her often got me tired too. It began to tell me how exhausted this leader was.

I asked her what she would say to a 15-year-old girl who is tired of working very hard preparing for her board exams?

I said to her, 'This young girl is very diligent and committed. She is bright and aspiring too. But she tends to really push herself very hard. Sometimes she works all day with her books'. I added that this girl was very obedient and only did what others asked of her—she never asked for what she wanted and always quietened herself from asking. I now asked the leader: 'If you were to be encouraging and kind to this kid, what would you tell her?'

This is what the leader said:

'Hi! You are very sweet. I believe you study all day and work so hard? You know rest and fun are very important for us. If you give yourself enough rest time, time to relax and have fun, won't you be happier? If you rest you will have much more energy to focus on your studies—believe me, try it. You will like it'.

With my encouragement the leader went on:

'You are so smart already. If you balance your work time and play, you will have more friends and you will have more fun. If people tell you to study you can always tell them that you need rest and fun too. You can tell them in a nice way what you would like'.

I was left smiling at her kindness and compassion to the little young girl. I asked her what would happen if she turns this same kindness and compassion to herself. She smiled, a light glaze of tears in her eyes. She said, 'I will come alive again'. It was a touching moment for us both.

She left the session realizing how tough she was with herself and that she can be kind to herself too. Cut herself some slack, quieten the inner critic chatter and put some relaxing joyful time for herself each week.

To use your internal Nurturing Parent ego state:

- Speak in kind words toward yourself. No put downs allowed!
- Replace judging language with encouraging language
- Offer yourself positive strokes each day
- Affirm and validate your strengths
- Tell yourself your needs are important
- Rest when you want

This state is within us and will need to remind ourselves to use it for ourselves!

The Adult ego state is another great ally to grow out of our adaptations. It develops with consistent effort from our side. Here are some ideas:

- Take on any form of either stillness, mindfulness or meditation practice. It builds the energy needed for being reflective

- Start journaling what you observe and notice more about yourself. It helps challenge old patterns that keep showing up

- Adopt curiosity as an attitude. Begin asking more questions to know more or to clarify

- Be direct. Express your thoughts and feelings in situations you may hesitate to

- Look for information that is relevant to the problem solving

- Do a course on critical thinking and writing

- Breathe and come into the present moment

Spend time with others who have a good potent Adult ego state

Am sure this chapter has shown you some limiting patterns that you recognize in yourself. Being aware and recognizing these adaptive patterns as well as the inner chatter within is the first step to change.

Practice 1

Write out what your parental voice says in these situations.

- When you wish to speak up and express your thoughts
- When you have fresh creative ideas and wish to share it with your team
- When you think of learning something new so you upskill yourself
- When you feel you want to venture out and learn something absolutely new
- When you want to either write a post on LinkedIn, a blog or an article
- When you wish to make a significant suggestion to a challenging client

Now for each of those statements ask these questions or have a friend ask you:

Is this really true? Is it absolutely true that I can't (influence others well/win an argument...)?

What would happen if I tried?

Do I know anyone else who might do it? What would they do?

What is the smallest step I can take now?

Affirming Ourselves

I personally resonate with the work of Louise Hay. Her book *Inner Wisdom: Meditations for the Heart and Soul* have wonderful affirming statements and an explanation for each. (7) Alternately pick any other affirmation approach and follow it daily.

Affirmations have the power to change our physiological make up at the cellular level and is a valuable tool for transformation as it activates our Nurturing Parent and our Adult state while the younger self in us can receive.

References

1. Berne Eric. *Transactional analysis in psychotherapy: The classic handbook to its principles.* New York, NY: Souvenir Press, 2001.

2. Stewart Ian and Joines Vann. *TA today: A new introduction to transactional analysis.* Nottingham and Chapel Hill, NC: Lifespace Publishing, 1987.

3. Goulding Robert and Goulding Mary. Injunctions, decisions and redecisions. *Trans Anal J* 1976; 6(1): 41–48.

4. Jongeward Dorothy. *Women as winners: Transactional analysis for personal growth.* Reading, MA: Addison-Wesley, 1981.

5. Day Anne and Vodarek Amy. *Good Enough: Embrace who you are, unleash your brilliance.* Canada: Full Circle Publishing, 2017.

6. Cuddy Amy. *Presence: Bringing your boldest self to your biggest challenges.* New York, NY: Little, Brown and Company, 2015.

7. Hay Louise. *Inner wisdom: Meditations for the heart and soul.* Carlsbad, CA: Hay House, 2000.

Chapter 4

RECLAIMING OUR POWER WITH GREENS

All the messages and behaviours that we have adopted over the years, through the Parent, Child and Adult ego states within us, show up in specific ways at work. They become a part of us and some of these messages and behaviours are limiting. Our observer is influenced with these messages and constantly shows up in our actions.

Some of the adaptation patterns mentioned in the previous chapter are part of the same overall story of messages that we have interwoven and adopted in our lives.

Leader who shied from the limelight

I coached a senior software quality manager. Her organization decided that they're going to organize a conference where they were going to host people from other organizations.

She put together a team and there was lot of material that she had to prepare and send out for the conference. She found that she was teamed up with three other guys and she was the only woman on the team. Somehow, she seemed to carry a major load of the conference duties. She took fabulous leadership in moving ahead. The conference started coming together and organizations were reached out to. There was lot of traction and action. The conference was a success and the colleagues pulled off a great job.

It was time, at the end of the conference, when the recognitions were about to happen. She said—'I don't know what happened but I just stepped back and allowed these three other colleagues to come forward to be seen and heard much more'. Right there, in front of the whole organization she lost a significant opportunity to be seen and heard.

The observer that she was, was telling her that—'You're not actually ready to be there in the front. Is it really that you've done so much? It looks like other people have done as much or more. Why are you stepping forward? What if you go there and fall flat on your face because you're going to be given the mic to speak?' The parent voice being critical of her showed up.

I believe that dealing with limiting messages in our personal narrative is a life skill. Why do I say it's a life skill?

Many times I have had people ask me: 'Don't you ever feel diffident and doubtful?' Of course, I do. As a person I've invested so much in myself and still the inner critic voice shows up. When it happens I say: 'Alright here it is again. Now let me see what I have to do with this!'

Investing in oneself is a very big blind spot for women as women make choices to invest in their family, kids and team, but do little to grow themselves as a human being.

Now these limiting messages show up in me less often than they did before. They show up in a quieter way. Their impact remains for much lesser time. But do they show up? Absolutely, they do. Understanding how to deal with this voice is important. Therefore, learning to recognize it as a voice and understanding how to quieten it is a skill that needs continual practice.

The Inner Critic

Tara Mohr, uses the term 'inner critic' in her book *Playing Big* to describe this inner voice that shows up time and again. I found her pointers on this very useful as she identifies the following situations where this critical voice shows up more often and louder. (1) Using her pointers, I have expanded on it highlighting the inner critic chatter.

- **It shows up when we need to put our deeply-held dreams and desires into action** in life or at work. 'This is the position I want to move to or maybe this is something that I want to start…' The desire is already born within us. The negative voice manifests and stops us. If we hesitate to listen, the tape will go on playing and perhaps the volume will get louder!

- It comes up **when we are in a tough spot and feeling low**. I was coaching a business leader who was in a bad patch personally. Her marital relationship was at risk. The voice would tell her: 'You are pathetic—you couldn't even make your marriage work!' When we're already in our delicate place it comes up and starts getting generalized into many other areas in our lives.

- It comes up when **we're at the edge of our comfort zone and we need to stretch**. A coachee I was working with was very successful. She had many years of solid HR experience and had grown well. She was now offered a position in a different place and she panicked. It would be a stretch for her personally and professionally. Being a married woman and never having led in a cross-cultural context, she was at her edge. She was very aware that staying on in the current role was not great. Yet, she declined the move saying she wasn't ready.

- It comes up when **we're creating a breakthrough or in a creative drift** making something new. I once met this lady who said that she was having such awful difficulties with her client company. People had been struggling for so long and suddenly she saw a ray of light in terms of changing a system, changing a process in how they were working. She believed this one innovation in how they worked would be a big breakthrough in terms of efficiency and productivity. But she found herself saying: 'Oh, who'd want to hear that? I better not bring it up. Am sure the client will shoot it down.'

- It also shows up **when we're attempting to design a new identity for ourselves**. I was talking to somebody who was a corporate professional. She wished to start her own business in health food. 'I want to be this bottle woman', she said. What's in these bottles? Sauces, preservatives, jams, ready-to-eat breakfast and ready-to-eat lunches. But she was in a completely different job context—in the financial sector. This would mean a big shift in identity. The voice said: 'Who is going to buy your bottles?' 'You are so ridiculous. You have no idea how to do this business.'

When does your critical voice show up? Do any of the above seem familiar?

The REDs and the GREENs

Here is a list of REDs or STOP messages—the voice of doubt, self-discount and devaluing. These are the adaptive patterns we have practised personally and professionally. They stop us from:

- Dreaming
- Aspiring

- Feeling confident
- Taking action
- Creating new possibilities

All of us have a bunch of REDs influenced by Parent ego state messages and Child ego state experiences. Every RED has a GREEN that we can use. The GREENs help us step out of our shadows and our self-limiting actions. They help us show up and reclaim our power. Every time we use a GREEN, it changes some aspect of our personality as we are practicing new behaviours.

The GREENs are the software updates we are making to our Parent, Adult and Child ego states. They are changes to the observer that we are. The GREENs are crafted by inspiration from Louise Hay's affirmations and books (2) as well as from the idea of permissions to ourselves that Eric Berne stated in TA literature. (3)

The GREENs support us in reclaiming our power to dream, act and create new possibilities for ourselves! I have illustrated how women have used their GREENs. As you go through it, select your GREENs to practice!

The GREENs throughout the book are new practices to integrate in your language, mood and behaviours! As you practice you will grow your strength. Practice is how we change.

All practice is the practice of making a turn in a different direction. —Karen Maezen Miller

---

1. RED: Don't be important

It is a variant of 'be quiet, don't be seen, don't be heard'. Another variant is 'others can be important, not you'.

Recognizing the RED: We are quiet and say little. We harbour self-doubt in how smart our ideas are. We hesitate before speaking and may be the last to speak in meetings.

We give in to others' needs, be it with a team or peers or even subordinates. (4)

We see glimpses of the same in our personal lives too. 95 per cent women in my courses share that they have experienced this sometime in their lives and they still feel this in certain domains of their life.

GREENs:

I will be seen.
I will show up more often.
I will acknowledge what I need.
I will ask for my needs to be met.

Vanitha decided to speak up in meetings and offered to lead them. She began monitoring her inner chatter to notice when she may be discounting herself and pulling back. This enabled her to acknowledge her needs at work or at home. Vanitha continues to be a little anxious each time she wishes to express herself. The GREEN 'I will be seen and heard' helps her share. She says it is having an impact as her team has begun to value her contributions.

Jennifer made time to exercise each day. Come what may, she asked for help at home so she could stay committed with this goal. It was her 'me time'. She had decided to make time for her health and the GREEN of 'I will ask for my needs to be met' was helping her each day.

---

2. RED: Don't think about

This could be about areas such as technology, finances, investing or budgeting for our business.

Another version of it is 'Stay small... stay dependent'.

Recognizing the RED: We stay confused and often say: 'I don't know'. We need to check all the time with others for their inputs and decisions. We distrust our thinking and criticize ourselves for our lack of capacity.

We may solve problems and number crunch in a certain domain in life like home but will remain dependent in domains connected to work and business. (4) The same is true for those of us who function in the technical field but do not challenge ourselves in skill or knowledge-building in technology.

GREENs:

I will take small steps and learn.
I will speak to other people who have crossed this bridge.
I will get a mentor or a coach who can guide me.
I will take charge.
There is always a first time.
I am capable of helping myself.

Veena was transitioning as an emerging leader into a business head. The message she carried was: 'You don't need to think about finances and budgets, and profit or loss'. How can one be a business unit head and not know how to interpret P&L statements?

She decided to take small steps—YouTubing a few videos to learn basics, meeting her CA every week to get briefed and ask a set of questions. Above all, she stopped delegating financial aspects to others and attended every meeting and decision personally. Small steps that she took were powerful.

In a workshop, a manager shared: 'My car broke down. I stopped in the middle of the road and I called my spouse and my dad'. She had paid for a two-year anywhere, anytime call-in facility with the car company. They could have come in and taken care of the car. It did not occur to her that she was limiting herself by acting small.

She decided that in areas that she depends on others, she will begin to take action herself. She began in simple places like knowing more about the different technology she uses. She began reading blogs and talking to others. In some aspects she wanted to make bigger shifts. She went to tech forums and addressed her questions, she researched and taught herself.

Above all, she gave herself permission to make mistakes and fail too.

She reminded herself that there is always a first time and it is okay.

---

3. RED: Speak only when you know it well (5)

Recognizing the RED: We speak up only when we are very knowledgeable, have no doubt on our competence and can never be wrong. Those of us following this will rarely express ourselves till we are a 100 per cent sure that we won't be criticized or challenged as we want to stay safe from humiliation or embarrassment. Speculative conversations are not our forte. Showing ourselves as fresh or exploring a domain as a learner is considered a poor show. So we rather keep quiet than bring forth our tentative thoughts on a topic. Instead, we may spend much time on research before sharing. At times, impactful ideas are lost in this waiting.

GREENs:

I can express my thoughts and feelings.
I can make mistakes and acknowledge them.
I can speculate and invite other people to think through with me.
I can share that I am in an exploration of ideas
I can be a dignified learner
All are beginners at some time in life.

Monica decided to work in the area of innovation. She had a very small team and an unclear mandate in her organization. Through coaching she decided that she cannot know everything in the technologies that they needed to use or explore further with. She shared with the team her idea of picking up few areas that the whole team could explore, study, and set up small prototypes and projects in. For that, the team would study areas and present them. She committed to being the first to offer two topics. She claimed that declaring herself a learner and an explorer was liberating as she dropped the anxiety that she needed to show up as an expert.

---

4. RED: Be pleasing please!

Recognizing the RED: Being pleasing, compliant, adaptive and nice is what we are constantly taught. (5) As a result we say 'yes' when we should be saying no. We can be quite overwhelmed from taking on too much and taking on others' work too. We have difficulty with assertive communication especially to those we see as significant and in a position of authority. We do not feel strong enough to hold our own in an argument. 'Peace at cost and no confrontation' is often our policy!

GREENs:

I will say what I need to say.
It's good for me to be direct.
At times I am going to please myself.
What I think and feel is important.
I value what I want.

'I will say what I need to say' a song by John Mayer became Ramani's anthem. She said she played this anthem each day on her way to work. It was such a creative and unique way of reinforcing this message for her. She felt over the months of practice that she has developed a strong spine and a strong voice that is surprising her manager.

---

5. RED: Don't relax

The variant is: 'Don't have fun, there is too much to do'. (4)

Recognizing the RED: When we have this RED we are uptight and can only think and talk about work. Teams can get burnt out with us, as we don't know how to relax and won't let them either. Many women believe they are being responsible and dutiful when they are in this 'always doing' mode. I know women who feel guilty when they are not working. They will even produce work when there isn't any. All for the compulsion of doing. We do not stop to ask 'What is this compulsive doing about?' 'What does it address or take care of?' Being in perpetual motion we feel purposeful and we don't have time to wonder about what else is possible for our life!

GREENs:

I can relax.
It's good for me to make time for myself.
Fun is good, let's have some fun.
Relaxing is caring for myself.

Maria led a team in a tech start-up. They functioned in a high intensity work schedule almost all year round. When Maria took her team on off-sites, it was usually packed through the day with meetings running into the night. In following this GREEN, she decided to lighten up the day schedule a little. She decided that evenings were to have fun. She left evenings free for the team or planned on a light activity that helps people bond over fun.

She began asking herself and her team—what fun activities were they planning over the weekend? She realized that making this change made her feel more connected to her team.

---

6.   RED: Don't ask for support

Recognizing the RED: We invest energy in appearing capable and not looking weak. (4)

Even if we are burdened, we will not easily ask for support nor will we delegate work. We do not want to be seen as inefficient and are happy to carry a lot, even at the cost of our health and peace of mind.

It isn't practical to imagine that we all are know-it-all persons. Asking is not a sign of inefficiency and we haven't learnt this.

GREENs:

I will ask for support when I need it.
I will actively do things with others so I share the burden.

Here are some super ideas on what women did with this GREEN as reported in the online Step Up course:

- Asking a college to be a sounding board for a business plan being created.
- Making a team member responsible for meeting agenda and documentation.
- Calling in the leader to support her in a tough customer call.
- Creating a small support team of three, the first time she wrote a tech proposal.
- Asking a colleague to run the team meeting while she could complete a research proposal.
- Organizing more house help—more hands the better.
- Training spouse and kids to take on specific home chores every day with a roster to guide all.

7. RED: Thinking and designing but no action

I have spoken to umpteen women who wish to start something new.

They sit at their desks, in coffee shops and at workshops with a book and paper making endless notes, plans about what is to be done. But they don't put these plans into action because they aren't good enough ... It's not practical enough ... or they need more detail. The problem of overthinking.

Recognizing the RED: We spend too much time creating a perfect plan. (5) A lot of learning can come through action and by designing through conversations. We design through inputs from others and make practical changes as we go along the way and have access to new inputs.

Action is one of the ways to receive feedback. This is what pilot and prototype style of design is all about. This GREEN is about getting out of your head and learn by doing. It is about getting into conversations with others so we design through stimulation, inputs, feedback and exchange of ideas.

GREENs:

As I walk the path appears for me.
I learn by doing.
I think well and solve issues as they come up
I can design by conversations with others
I can start with small steps and move ahead
Enough help and support is available to me

Meera was a therapist. She wished to create a series of programmes on parenting and children. She was stuck with creating her perfect plan for over one year with no action.

She used this GREEN to write up a plan for module 1 and 2. She got a group and ran it announcing that it was a pilot. She put up large charts in the workshop and used post-its to collect ideas from parents on what they wanted to learn about. These charts gave her the plans for module 3–6. She then designed those and ran them. At every stage, she took feedback and incorporated it. Over a year, she had a robust 6-module course and felt a sense of accomplishment.

Her core mantra was: I learn as I go forward.

---

8. RED: Not showing 'me'

Another variation of this is 'Leaving myself out'.

Recognizing the RED: If we are presenting then we talk views, opinions and theories. We do not bring our personal view or experience into the conversation as a way of illustrating or sharing.

Another way of being unimportant and insignificant. (4) At times we share others' views, as though we need scaffolding and justification to make our voice sound credible. What about our unique experience and thinking? Can we begin to value our own voice too? Bringing one's own experience, story and thinking into a conversation is a sign of valuing oneself, reflection and trust in our thinking. In my training to be a teacher in psychotherapy this was a big learning step for me which has added power to my speaking assignments in a big way!

This is also true when we are in meetings where there is a view being demanded. Many of us google or look for the experts view. As we lead, it is useful for us to do an enquiry into our values, what we stand for and what our opinion is on current matters.

GREENs:

My thinking is good, I will speak it.
My thinking is as important as others.
My voice is unique and it is my own.
My story has value and meaning.
My story connects to why I care about something.
My story connects me to others.

An architect shared her story: She was invited to speak at a forum. She had prepared a nice presentation on a challenging project and an innovation she had made on the project. She felt her presentation was too technical and began to feel distant from it. She kept thinking that it had all the details that were impressive, and yet something was missing.

She decided to share what she deeply cared about in her field of architecture and how it connected to the purpose behind her project. She decided to put into her talk—stories of significant challenges and how it impacted her and her team. Including her experience, her emotional responses to it and her thinking process, lifted the presentation to another level.

She communicated with conviction and the audience connected to her very well. She made the entire project very real which enhanced her public identity.

---

9. RED: You need to know more, you are still not ready.

A variant is: 'You need to learn more, study more and get another qualification perhaps'.

Girls often get lot of strokes for being a good student, learning well. Sheryl Sandberg referred to this in her TED talk when she spoke of how girls prepare for exams and their feedback on when they believe they have finished versus how boys who always seem to think they are prepared. (6)

Recognizing the RED: This is about never feeling ready.

Tara Mohr in her book *Playing Big* calls it 'Good student habits'. (1) The result is that we are endlessly joining courses and polishing our skills out of fear that we are not good enough. We believe the extra credential is essential. In today's volatile and unpredictable environment, there is only that much that a formal course can give you. The biggest gift we can give ourselves is the skill of learning as we are growing.

At times we believe we are committed to quality and a standard, and that a new credential will give us just that. We need to pay attention to whether it is actually required, or if we are just giving ourselves an excuse to mask our fears.

For example, if we decide to implement a new idea, we decide that we need to read at least three more books, research ten other websites or talk to a couple of more people. We get into an endless cycle of 'preparation' instead of putting the idea into action.

GREENs:

I learn as I do.
Practical learning and action has value.
I have what it takes and I will start from where I am.
All big journeys start with a small step.
I am enough as I am and I will keep learning.
I am good enough.
I have strengths and gifts I can use.
I keep updating myself.

A lady in one of my workshops told me she was contacted by a recruiter who spoke to her of a head HR position. She shared: 'I felt so diffident. I think I am not ready at all'.

She mentioned that she told the recruiter she is not interested and that she will pass on numbers of other colleagues who may be keen. As we went through this content on the course she was both amazed and embarrassed! Using her GREEN, she decided to call the recruiter and say that she gave it a rethink and she would like to apply for the position.

I personally created Step Up, my online course, from a place of not knowing. My GREEN is that I learn as I do. I already know enough to begin. As I continue to learn, I will add increased value in what I offer.

---

10. RED: Going alone. Being a solo act

This is true for entrepreneurs, small business owners and corporate professionals too.

Recognizing the RED: If we have an idea, we do not easily share it. We do not find collaborators and see that in togetherness there is much more that is possible. We do not value networking. We work a lot by ourselves.

Being with others is natural to us women from the time we were hunter-gatherers and caretakers! Generations of women stayed back and worked together to take care of home. With each other they shared fears, their joys and found solutions to their problems. It comes naturally to us to thrive when we are together. This is the basis of women's circles all over the world.

We need to learn the skills of collaboration and the skill to have speculative conversations. We need to allow ourselves to lean in, explore and take risks together with others. We can drop any insecurity around other talented women and develop the abundance that there is place for all of us to bring our unique gifts to the world.

GREENs:

Belonging with others is good.
I can align with others who share an interest in what I care about.
I can build a network of support and care.
I can learn and grow with others.
With others I can do more than what I can do alone.
Collaboration brings me energy, drive and creativity.

I would like to share my own story here. In the last few years almost all my work has been collaborative. This wasn't the case before. As a psychotherapy teacher and supervisor, I collaborate with other colleagues at my level and sometimes even at levels junior to mine. For the last few years more than 50 per cent of my work has been in the collaborative space. I find that it is refreshing to have creative ideas and new ways of thinking and executing with other people.

As a leadership coach, I have collaborated with other coaches to facilitate workshops as well as webinars. Collaboration is an effort as it takes time to develop trust and ways of working that suits everyone involved. However, collaborations have brought huge gifts for me in the form of support, new learning, new ideas, the capacity to deliver bigger and complex projects, as well as to enhance the creative think tank.

The more I learnt to articulate what I wanted and why I wanted to collaborate, and the more I was willing to speculate with others what each person would bring to the game, the more I became comfortable to play. Last year there were several online events I ran collaboratively with women leaders and coaches from India and other countries.

If you have picked your GREENs I urge you to journal where, how, when and with whom you can bring these GREENs alive at work each day. As we practise the GREENs, they become more ingrained into our new observer, thereby generating new actions and new results for us.

My experience as a coach shows me that those who stay committed to their GREENs and use them as mantras for growing themselves, make a huge difference in their leadership within a one year period. Countless coachees and participants on my courses now tell me how these GREENs are second nature to them and that they are thrilled to be finally making an impact in their leadership.

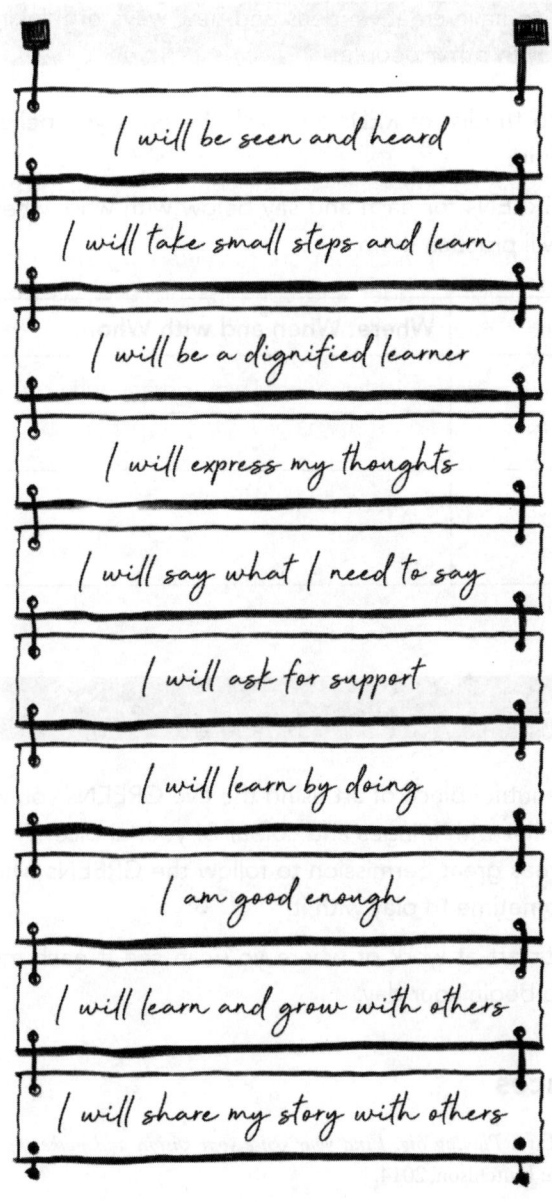

I will be seen and heard

I will take small steps and learn

I will be a dignified learner

I will express my thoughts

I will say what I need to say

I will ask for support

I will learn by doing

I am good enough

I will learn and grow with others

I will share my story with others

Reclaiming our powers through green practices

Practice 1

Go back to the list of REDs and pick the ones you believe are stopping you.

Pick the GREENs for each and say below with who, where and how you will practice them

GREENs	Where, When and with Whom

Practice 2

Make a beautiful piece of art using the five GREENs you wish to practice. Fill it with images and colour of your choice. The Child ego state has great permission to follow the GREENs when it is allowed sometime to play with it!

Pin up your art at work or where you can see it each morning before you begin your day.

References

1.   Mohr Tara. *Playing big: Find your voice your vision and make this happen.* London: Hutchison, 2014.

2.   Hay Louise. *Inner wisdom meditations for the heart and soul.* Carlsbad, CA: Hay House, 2000.

3. Berne Eric. *What do you say after you say hello.* New York, NY: Grove Press, 1972.

4. Goulding Robert and Goulding Mary. Injunctions, decisions and redecisions. *Trans Anal J* 1976; 6(1): 41–48.

5. Kahler Taibi and Capers Hedges. The Miniscript. *Trans Anal J*, 1974; 4(1): 26–42.

6. Sandberg Sheryl. Why we have too few women leaders. TED: Ideas worth spreading, TED Women, 2010. https://www.ted.com/talks/sheryl_sandberg_why_we_have_too_few_women_leaders?

Chapter 5

DESIGN YOUR FUTURE

Sarla had a new idea for a while now. She wanted to start an enterprise in the corporate gifting arena. Her talents and keen interest in fine arts, design and craft had sparked this new proposition. Although she had a steady job in the accounts department of a pharmaceutical company, she knew her heart was elsewhere. But she was hesitant to take any action. Her fears were holding her back. Running a business meant a lot of time and energy that would need to be spent outside home. Besides, a business was considered riskier than a predictable 9–5 job.

I met Prisca on a train journey. She sat opposite me, a young college student. I struck a conversation with her, asking about her studies and future plans. Prisca very excitedly explained her Bachelor of Arts degree and her plans to travel the world, do a course on tourism and become a tour guide. Her father had advised her to do a Montessori course and become a teacher.

Why? It would be easier to get a teacher's job anytime or anywhere. It would demand less of her and would be easy for her family to find a suitable marriage alliance for her. What if Prisca's family had different thoughts for her future from the ones she held?

Vimal, a manager in a software company and a mother of two girls was a fabulous cook. She had innovative ideas and wanted to start a health food company that would cater from home. Yet, she held herself back. Her husband ran a printing business. Her job would bring a steadier income. Wouldn't it be a risk for both of them to run businesses? What would her family think of this? Was she risking the future of her children?

Vera felt like she needed a challenge. Her work as a team leader was great, but she knew she could perform better in a customer-facing role. This would mean a lot of travel for days, sometimes weeks, visiting client sites. But would that mean she'd have to shirk her household responsibilities? What if it upsets the status quo at home? She thought it was better to forget this idea.

These stories sound familiar, don't they?

Culture, family of origin and the way girls are socialized in our society—all of these reasons lead to certain assessments that we as women, begin to hold about ourselves and the world around us. They begin to define what we need to care about. Often, it is others who have defined for us what we need to care about. We have unknowingly adopted those ideas and believed them to be ours as we have not consciously examined them.

When I was introduced to the idea of care,[1] it had a profound impact on me and continues to be the core of my self-enquiry.

What Is Care?

Bob Dunham explains care as that which energizes us. It is at the root of purpose. It can be at the root of action and can be life-giving. It sheds light on that which is really significant and important to us.[2]

There are some important care questions we need to ask ourselves. A more expanded list to explore your cares is at the end of this chapter.

What are the core concerns for my life?
What do I care about with regard to my family? My career? My life?
Why do I care about these?
Am I taking care of what I care about?
What am I willing to give up to choose my care?

My work with women has revealed that many women are scared to have what I call the 'Care conversation' with themselves. We hesitate to ask ourselves: 'What do I really care about most?' We are afraid it may rock either the family boat, the marriage boat or the professional boat for that matter.

While organizations offer diversity and women in leadership initiatives to women professionals, my work has highlighted for me

---

[1] Care is one of the key distinctions of leadership and I have learnt the primacy of care and its meaning from my teacher Bob Dunham in the Coaching Excellence in Organizations programme organized by the Institute for Generative Leadership, USA. He has also referred to this in his paper 'The Generative Foundations of Action in Organizations: Speaking and Listening' published in the *International Journal of Coaching in Organizations*, 2009.

[2] Bob Dunham has referred to this in his paper 'The Generative Foundations of Action in Organizations: Speaking and Listening' published in the *International Journal of Coaching in Organizations*, 2009.

Care is the root of purpose, action and satisfaction.
Care is the root of the future we want for ourselves
Take care of what you care about
-Bob Dunham

that as women, many of us have buried our aspirations so deep that we have forgotten that they exist. Forgetting our dreams has helped us live our lives and work according to expected social norms. This has been at a tremendous cost to our connection with the self and our unique gifts and capabilities which remain hidden to the world.

What would happen if women began to ask these questions?

Is there a way for us to care about our family, our relationships as well as manage a professional care?

Asking ourselves what we care about can be scary. It can upset status quo. But it can also bring unexpected gifts into our lives so we can grow to our fullest potential.

Why Delve into the Care Question?

Cares are connected to a future that we want for ourselves and others too. At times this future sits inside of us, unarticulated or in some cases, unacknowledged even. To have this future that we wish, we need to make new choices in life.

However, care is not just about our choices. It is that which we deeply resonate with. It gives us meaning and purpose in our life. It brings us value and satisfaction each day. For Sarla, it was about starting a new business in art and design. For Prisca, it was about becoming a tour guide and travelling. Where do we see ourselves deeply involved and happy? This is an important question to ask ourselves.

Care leads to purposeful activity. It is connected to action in a way that it energizes us towards doing a set of things.

Care is 'fundamental dimension to all our actions'.[3]

We may be connected to our cares or disconnected. If we are connected, we produce actions, and hence create results in that domain.

Focus on my care

Many years ago, my daughter who was then five years old, was going through a tough time at school. Her cognitive and social functioning was not at the same level as kids of her age. She could not cope with school activities relevant to her age.

[3] See footnote 5.

I found a neurological programme in United States which could help her overcome this difficulty. We needed to take her out of school, go to United States and train ourselves in this programme. Following this, we had to run a home programme for her 24/7 back here in India. This would enable a change in her neurological health.

I had hit a speed breaker with this. I had to make a choice. During this time, I was running two organizations in partnership with a colleague. I loved my work and had aspirations to grow it in a significant way. I had reached a fork in the road. I had to choose.

I remember having a conversation with my coach and hearing the important learning I needed at that moment. He said: 'Taking care of your daughter is important right now. Taking care of your care is a leadership move and you need to make it. Do what is important in the moment'.

I figured that I cared about my child and her growth perhaps at a higher level than I cared about my business. She was at a developmental stage of her life, where her issue could not wait to be attended to. My career could. This reflection allowed me to lean towards what I cared about. Allowing myself to get centred deeply in my care was important for me.

This gave me and the entire family energy to gear up for the next two years. I wound up my two organizations, quit work and went off the market. My home became a lab—with gym mats, massage tables, breathing machines and contraptions that allowed us to dive into the neurological programme in full swing. We were scraping the bottom of our savings to sponsor several of our visits to United States to diagnose my daughter, as well as to be trained to work with her. After an arduous amount of work for 18 months, my daughter went back to school. She was reading, writing and functioning almost at the level that she needed to at her age.

I cared about the health of my child and I wanted to be instrumental in changing it. Not doing it would mean a certain future for my daughter and I did not wish that future.

I wished a future where she would flourish and be able to do what most kids her age could. It connected deeply to myself, as a woman and as a mother. It guided my choices and actions so that I could take care of what mattered to me.

I asked the Care questions again in two years' time, and this time the answers were different from those I found earlier. My cares had changed as life had changed and so had I. I decided to go back to work and set out to do all that I dreamt of professionally!

Our cares keep changing and the Care questions are one of my favourites that I keep going back to. Infact, what we care about as a family is an important question for me. Each year we unfailingly review this and allow it to guide where we wish to put our energy each year.

Action, Action Action ... or Just Activity?

If we stay disconnected with our cares, we may be in action, but it is more likely just mindless, routine activity, in my opinion. It is not addressing something we care about.

Pragya worked as a project manager in a tech company. She was talented, successful and had landed a dream project. Still, she felt restless in her job and could not understand why.

Pragya's bookshelves at home were filled with books on child care, child education and early children's development. Her weekends and holidays were spent visiting early year schools, interacting with teachers and visiting conferences connected with education.

Her actual care wasn't a career in technology. Her care lay with children and their education. She had not yet understood or articulated it for herself. This area of early childhood education was where she spent her time and energy joyfully.

Nikita was an architect. She led a team of designers and mainly executed commercial and housing projects. But a spark would light up her eyes when anyone mentioned community living projects to her. Developing structures that already existed within communities and enhancing community living spaces was where her care lay. She would volunteer to be part of those projects even though it paid her nothing. She cared about using design skills for a community. She had not yet articulated this. Yet, it already guided her actions. What would happen if Nikita knew with great clarity her care on community-based architecture? How would it change her actions?

Vinitha worked as a financial analyst. She had a 10-year career behind her and was doing very well. She was slated for a promotion too. She was the happiest when she spent time volunteering at a women's shelter—a place that provided temporary living for women in distress. Along with providing skill development programmes that equipped these women with skills that would open livelihood opportunities, Vinitha was great at talking to them, comforting them and guiding them through their problems. In a course, while working with me she recognized her connection with her care of counselling and being of service to people. This motivated her and she decided to spend three evenings a week and every weekend feeding this care.

Reflection and a call to meaningful action for yourself:

- You may be working hard in careers that do not energize you anymore.

- You may be shaping your career in an area you were educated in, but now do not feel excited about anymore.

- You are spending long hours with a very busy calendar full of meetings and chasing goals that don't matter very much to you.

- You may even be recognized for your achievements at work but you find the reward lacks significance.

- You may have a goal sheet pasted on your soft board at work and yet you are procrastinating several actions towards those goals.

- You experience low energy often.

- You experience a feeling of conflict inside yourself all the time—when you are in one place you feel you should be elsewhere doing something else.

- You may feel joy in a certain activity but then you tell yourself you are wasting time as you've not come this far in life to throw away all that you have worked for till now.

If any of the above points seem familiar, I invite you to take time and explore your cares at the end of this chapter.

When we connect with our cares, we are motivated. We experience satisfaction, find meaning and use our time to feed our cares.

Taking Care of What You Care about: Design Your Life

I think care is connected to meaning and satisfaction in life. When we are not taking care of what is important to us, we become dissatisfied and restless.

It is not uncommon that we live our lives in ways I have described above. We work hard at a job or a career. We are even successful. Yet, we do not stop to ask:

- Is this what I really care about? How come?

- What future am I creating for myself? Does that future matter?

- If it does not take care of the future that I want, then why am I doing this?

- Is there something else I need to do instead?

- What will this set of actions take me towards? Is that future exciting and expansive for me?

When I say future, I am envisioning one that we care about and one that is exciting. Care evokes a sense of joy, satisfaction, comfort and an expansiveness in us. It is this deep connection to the essence within ourselves that is at the heart of leadership presence, leadership voice and how we are seen by others too.

Knowing our care allows us to feel a few inches taller. It allows us to speak with clarity and conviction. The world begins to see us as purposeful in our actions.

Care is connected to designing our future.
Aligning with our cares changes the actions we take.
These actions take us towards a future that matters to us.

Sara loved meeting her friends. Every Saturday she met up with them, had a few drinks, ate all that she wanted and 'partied hard' in her own words. She spent each weekend filled with action until late hours. The following day she would not be able to wake up or exercise. Sometimes, she did this even on weekdays, and it became difficult for her to get to work on time.

As months passed, she put on weight, developed blood pressure and aching knees. Occasionally, she became concerned about her weight, and would decide to eat healthier. But this did not last long and she would go back to her old ways. Ameeta was moving towards a future that had ill health and fatigue.

Sara was in one of my courses, and realized to her horror that she was moving fast towards a future that was scary. She was 31 and had health problems. She decided that health was going to be her care, and a significant one. She decided that she needed a buddy to keep her accountable. She worked out with a friend that she would make a call to each day and report her actions taken for her health. She changed her diet, altered her habits for her weekends and even decided that for some time, she needed to stay away from friends and activities that dragged her towards her old patterns. At the end of eight months, she reported with pride and joy about the benefits of her new actions. She even shared that she was on the before–after advertising of the gym she had enrolled in! She was now an inspirational story to others!

She volunteered in one of my leadership courses and shared the above experience with pride. She mentioned how her self-esteem is increasing each day, as she is taking care of her health in the way she wanted to. She believes this is self-leadership! She shared: 'Every woman needs to create a space for herself and that comes from understanding and being aware of who she is. I believe that every person is a leader. Within the space of day-to-day responsibilities, we can choose to step up to the life we want to live by saying: "These are things I care about and this what I would like to do"'.

Attention Needs to Follow Care

We have cares in personal and professional domains. Being clear about our cares is a leadership practice. Knowing and articulating them not only heightens our energy, but also impacts those around us, including work teams, family and business partners.

Knowing our cares helps us make choices about where to focus our energy and time. As humans we are finite and time is finite too. We need to choose where we can put our energy and time as it concerns the future we are designing for ourselves, our families and our organization. Attention needs to follow care.[4]

[4] See footnote 5.

Here are few examples of big cares that women decided in their professional domains. Each of these were followed up with clear actions that these leaders held themselves accountable to.

- Building a competent team with diverse skills.
- Leading through thought leadership for business.
- Changing the customer satisfaction indicators at least three points upwards.
- Handling all investment decisions for the organization and leading those discussions.
- Being the go-to person for all technical architecture issues in their businessline.
- Developing three second-in-commands in a school by the end of the year.
- Functioning as a thought leader in the development sector.
- Contributing at a strategy level to business whereby, over 50 per cent of the new value ideas come from their team.
- Establishing XYZ modality of education and learning as a valuable approach at the national level in India.
- Launching oneself as an HR partner and make a full movement from the technical space to HR.
- Establishing oneself as a designer of repute by focussing on the sustainability of design.

Below are three practices I offer you.

100 per cent of the women in my leadership courses report that these are one of the biggest and wisest investments of time they have ever made. Many of them say it was life changing!

Practice 1

We live life in many of the following dimensions. Some of us have cares that lie in these different dimensions.

Some domains to reflect on are:

- Family
- Relationships
- Home
- Finances
- Health
- Spiritual
- Learning and growth
- Performance—in which domain?
- A social issue
- Career
- Community

Questions to reflect:

- Identify some domains you wish to examine for yourself.
- In those domains ask yourself what is currently going good.
- Reflect on what aspect could be more effective and why does that higher effectiveness matter.
- Identify in each domain, one small step you can change to help you take care of that care more effectively. Support yourself to start small.

Practice 2

This is a reflection and journaling practice which you may do over few days.

Sit in a quiet place and write out your responses to these questions.

Be uncensored and honest with yourself.

If it helps you to explore these through conversations with another person, do seek out a friend or mentor.

Step 1

- Do you know what wakes you up in the morning?
- What really matters to you in life? List it.
- Ask yourself: 'Where do I spend the most time?' Making a time inventory can be very revealing.
- What produces energy, satisfaction and meaning for you?
- Are you familiar with the feeling of doing something that brings you alive? What is it?
- Do you have gifts and strengths? Are you using them?
- Are you doing what you love to do and it energizes you at work?
- Think about the future you want to have—your future includes all of your life and your work. Describe how life and work fit in that future.

Step 2

From your responses above I am sure a picture has emerged and some key areas of focus too.

- Each of our cares is like a big umbrella. Under each care we take several actions to take care of that care of ours. From your reflections above, identify three top cares.

- Now note what outcome do you desire in each of those domains of care? List two–three outcomes under each care.

- Ask yourself: 'Am I willing to dedicate my time and energy to it?'

- Each week, each day, what are you going to do to take care of these cares?

- What other activity will I need to give up to make time for my cares?

Practice 3

Pick up your professional care. Maybe it is changing your client satisfaction numbers, building technical expertise, or creating a rock solid delivery team.

Imagine this professional care as an umbrella. Name it clearly.

An umbrella has four–five spokes that hold the structure in place. Similarly your care umbrella also has such spokes.

Name the key spokes and actions you need to take for each spoke to be strong.

Ask yourself how you are doing with these actions, what do you need to change in your day, your relationships and your working process so you attend to the actions you need to take.

Is there someone at work—maybe a supportive peer, a manager or anyone else you can share this with? What happens for you as you do that?

Keep visiting these three practices twice a year as a part of your stepping up journey.

Cares are a map and navigating with a map keeps us on track towards our destination.

DESIGN EFFECTIVE ACTION

When I talk to people and ask them: 'What gives us results?' their response is: 'Actions give us results. We do xyz set of things and we get results'.

An individual, a team or an organization produces results because of the set of actions we take individually or collectively.

In whatever context we are in, be it leadership at work or at home, we often need others to take action on something we care about and something that they care about too. But most often, we do not get the results we need. We may not even see the necessary action that we expected.

Anatomy of Action model[1] powerfully explains the connection between care, commitments, actions and results. Not just any kind of result, but results that matter and results that take care of something significant for us.

---

[1] Anatomy of Action is a creation of Bob Dunham. He has referred to the Anatomy of Action in several of his papers, some unpublished. He has also referred to this in his paper 'The Generative Foundations of Action in Organizations: Speaking and Listening' published in the International Journal of Coaching in Organizations, 2009

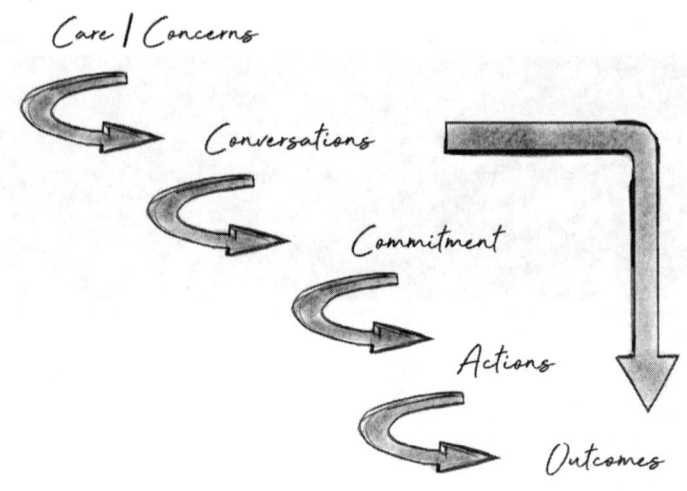

Care / Concerns

Conversations

Commitment

Actions

Outcomes

Anatomy of Action

Pic copyright 2008, Bob Dunham

Results Come from Being in Action

Without action there can be no outcomes or results. Simply performing some activity also does not generate results. Relevant action is important to generate desired results. The thoughts we hold behind these actions are important too. Thinking that is positive and options-oriented, open possibilities for action. 'I can, I will'; 'Let me try this, let me take a small step...' are all thoughts that open possibilities.

Action Comes from Commitments

When we are at official meetings or anywhere else, we see that people are committing to something. They say: 'Yes I will do this' or 'No I cannot'. Sometimes these commitments are clear and sometimes not. They may be commitments with conviction or commitments with hesitation. Commitments made with hesitation, demotivation and in helplessness cannot and should not be treated as valid commitments. However, when we 'read' in the body language of the other that a commitment is made with conviction by sharing facts and clear timelines, we know we have a good enough commitment. From those commitments come relevant action.

Commitments Are Shaped within Conversations

Commitments include thought and emotion of the person making it. A choice to say 'yes' includes thinking and feeling. Powerful and effective conversations lead to strong commitments that we can trust.

Powerful and effective conversations include conversations where we pay attention to the complete bodily interaction we are having with others. Some aspects we must pay attention to in good conversations are:

- Using our 'listening' to pay attention to their body language.
- Examining our thoughts and others' contributions.
- Listening for underlying thoughts and emotions—ours and others.
- Checking for supportive data vis-à-vis a topic or the individual concerned.
- Sensing hesitations and incompleteness in what we are speaking.

In a conversation, all this requires using a range of skills for listening and understanding.

We can think back now to meetings that went on for long and had very little action or very little commitment come out of them. Meetings are a type of conversation.

On the other hand, we can also recollect other conversations either with an individual or a group of people that were so fully alive, that lots came out of it in terms of commitments and action.

Powerful conversations often give rise to clear commitments. So, conversations are generative. The word 'generative' is used because conversations generate commitments, actions and new possibilities.

Santhya Vikram, the founder of Yellow Train school in Coimbatore, shares this about conversations.

'I read somewhere that you are never the same after reading a beautiful book, or watching a touching movie or after listening to a lovely piece of music. The same is true of a good conversation. A good conversation clarifies your own ideas, it resounds what lies in the innermost depths of your heart. It sometimes mirrors all your doubts and confusions. Sometimes, it is great validation. Sometimes what appears fuzzy like dust becomes more real with flesh and wings. At other times, it challenges you to think further and stretches your boundaries and beliefs.

If I look at the evolution of the Yellow Train school, I have had every one of these kind of conversations in coaching. Powerful questions have been the most defining aspect of these con-versations. Some of the questions have been most directional, and have led to an emergence of a certain kind of thinking. As a leader it has shaped many of my raw ideas, given me a reality check often, broken my old and limiting beliefs, they have expanded my capabilities and provided me with what was necessary around each bend of the road. From this place I have made some really big commitments to self, to my team and the parent community'.

Care Powers our Conversations

Care clarifies the purpose and reason for why we are in the conversation. When we own and acknowledge our reasons, it shines through to the other.

Expressing our care actively in conversations clarifies why commitments are required from the other. It clarifies the nature of the commitments needed and how those commitments fit into a bigger picture that we hold. It shows others their part in our game, and perhaps our part in theirs. It clarifies why the task has relevance to us.

Care brings meaning into conversations. As humans, we are meaning-making beings. The meanings we make bring us value, satisfaction and comfort. It is for this reason we make commitments in conversations.

Care brings meaning into conversations and relationships. As humans, we are meaning-making beings. The meanings we make bring us value, satisfaction and comfort.

Just as how our spinal cord is not a discretionary structure—we do not get to decide the number of vertebrae in it. The Anatomy of Action is one such non-discretionary structure with each element having its place and significance in creating outcomes in our lives.

By that, I mean that we cannot skip some parts of it and imagine that we will get actions. If we do omit parts of the Anatomy, we can safely assume that the actions may be coming from the others' need to comply or from a place of fear.

Without conversations, action from others may also come because they share the same care or have similar values as us. As leaders, we need to analyse and ask if actions in our team or from another individual are coming from a place of fear or a place of will and clarity.

Care conversation in the personal domain

I was concerned about my daughter's nutrition, weight and health. The outcome I needed was for her to take care of her health in a responsible manner—that she ate what her body needed, had balanced meals and had the energy to do all that she wanted to do as a young dynamic student. Of course, this isn't easily done when you are speaking to a teenager.

I needed to start with my care—not just as a mother but also a care as to why health is significant in enabling a better life for her. Many conversations later, including some emotional ones where I expressed my fears and anxieties as a parent, I began to see commitment.

Not including my emotional state would have been a missing conversation between a mother and daughter. I am glad I did not hesitate to express my fears and concerns to her.

Slowly and steadily I began seeing a shift in her approach to nutrition, exercise and a routine. This lead to assurance and happiness, not just for me but for the entire family. Getting a teenager to shift from a careless attitude towards health, to one of will and resolve is a fulfilling experience as a parent. Now, we tease her that we have much to learn from her because she stays so committed to her health. I continue to marvel at my daughter and her committed actions that generated the outcomes that she wanted for her health. Moreover, I am glad for the conversations that enabled me to motivate her to get responsible for her own health and future.

Care conversation in the professional domain

A few years ago, I recollect wanting to begin offering webinars. I had no experience in setting up webinars till then. I was attending a conference in United States at the time and I decided to seek the support of three other colleagues, who were also present at the conference, in coaching. I decided to share my care on offering women in India a possibility of flexibility in learning and access to learning content that suited them.

I was speaking to three women coach colleagues from Canada, Mexico and United States who didn't altogether understand the Indian context of how women functioned within the multiple roles or responsibilities in their lives. This needed to be explained along with why I thought webinars would make a difference with many more women being able to access this work. The three other coaches and I had a shared care on women leadership, and once they were aligned with my care the project began shaping up. We decided to offer a series of webinars on multiple topics free of cost, to women who were keen on learning. The idea was to begin to test the technology medium and check responses for people's interest in this offer as well as the method of learning.

The following year we went ahead and offered these webinars which were overbooked in 48 hours and we received much appreciation. My colleagues allowed me to hold space for the whole process as I helped set the cultural context for the entire group. The same year, the same team of four coaches, me included, also offered similar webinars to women in the United States and Mexico. Having a care conversation changed the motivation and energy of the lead coaches. It shaped the offer we made, it also shaped how we rolled it out. They began to see why this was important to me and they were able to align and work with me in a mood of great curiosity, generosity as well as ambition.

What Can Go Wrong with the Anatomy of Action?

Missing and Incomplete Conversations

In some relationships there are missing conversations.[2] These are conversations that matter but are not happening between two individuals, within a team or in an organization. They're hidden because people hold negative assessments around raising issues. Sometimes there is fear or anxiety about the issue. People also hold internal conversations within themselves which they do not wish to make public.

Nicole is one of the quality management leaders of a large software project. There has been a constant stream of problems on the projects, despite several calls and meetings being scheduled with the customer. Her manager does not invite her onto these calls. Instead, he calls her colleague Raghav, who is another leader on the project. Nicole is left with several questions in her mind such as: 'Why am I not invited?'; 'Does he find me falling short of my work in some way?'; 'Have I done something wrong in my role as a leader?'; 'Why is someone else being asked details when I need to be asked?'; 'Is Raghav more competent a lead than I am?'

However, she does not ask these questions to her manager. She continues to work resentfully and keeps doubting herself at every stage.

---

[2] I heard these ideas from Bob Dunham in the Coaching Excellence in Organizations programme organized by the Institute for Generative Leadership, USA. He has referred to this in his paper 'The Generative Foundations of Action in Organizations: Speaking and Listening' published in the *International Journal of Coaching in Organizations*, 2009.

Each of us has faced a similar situation as Nicole at some point in our careers. We're hesitant and afraid to bring the private conversation out of our heads and lay it out on the table. Instead we sometimes make up our own story to explain what could be happening to us. We may even forget that we made the story to fill the gaps as we did not have enough information to understand what is going on at work!

Example of missing conversations at work could be:

- Why am I not put into meetings that are customer-facing?
- Why am I not rated the top in this project? What is missing?
- What is the standard held in our teams for superior performance?
- What culture are we building when leaders do not practise what they ask others to do?
- Why don't we have a better structure to our meetings?
- Why are we so confused about roles and responsibilities in our organization?

Conversations are *ineffective and incomplete* when no attention is paid to details that need discussion. At times we may be having a second line of thought which is not voiced. Other times we don't ask the right questions that we should be asking out of fear of looking naive and ignorant. At times we have a gut feeling that we don't listen to and do not address in a conversation.

Sometimes we are blindly receiving what the other person is saying. We accept without questioning, we are not listening to specific elements or even data that is missing. At times people communicate vaguely or at too a high a level with no practical specifics that we need to hear and yet we let it go without clarifying. There are times when someone is asking us for commitments on tasks where they have not defined timelines clearly or have not explained what standards of performance or quality have to be met. This is a good place to complete an incomplete conversation by asking questions to clarify and be clear about what would satisfy the other.

I have had several women share that they experience diffidence in having these conversations because they believe they may appear as though they are criticizing or asking too many questions unnecessarily. Many women speak of their lack of negotiation for fair compensation. Compensation can be seen as a missing conversation regarding the standards being used to decide salaries or raises. Standards that organizations use to decide salaries or what a high performance is, is in itself a missing conversation. It can also be seen as a missing conversation on parity especially when some of them have data of what a male colleague with similar competence and contribution is being compensated.

When I have had conversations with women in public sector organizations, they share how rampant the action of promoting a male colleague over a female is. Women who ask too many questions are viewed as a nuisance and as aggressive.

Notice how easily we fall back into adapted patterns of being nice and adjusting, and not wanting to rock the boat. We fall into patterns of being passive and doing nothing even in the face of unfairness. It continues to be difficult to call out what needs to be seen and acknowledged.

Completing conversations effectively and basing our commitments on understanding what is required of a task or an individual, is an act of being responsible. It is an act of commitment that we ask questions and clarify, that we even bring up issues that may lie under the surface. It is an act of caring for what the other cares about. It lies within your commitment to the task at hand, the team and that individual.

When we are committed to our care of growing ourselves into potent leaders, we must bring ourselves to have missing conversations—be it with our leaders, teams or significant stakeholders. There may be an unconscious bias at play and calling out a disparity or a bias may set right many things as covert issues are now made overt.

Care: Yours and Mine

Karen and Kay's story

I was once in a long coaching relationship with Karen, a woman leader in Africa. She had recently taken over as head of the country's operations in her company and was introduced to Kay—one of her reportees, who had been in the organization for the last eight years. This reportee led one of the key accounts of a large customer.

Kay's clients had escalated issues to the management. Karen expressed being 'locked out' of Kay's account. She found it hard to get information from the team, and to access documentation and meeting notes. Digging deep into Kay's team, Karen found many anomalies in how Kay was managing the team, in the statistics of the account and the client had issues with her as well.

I presented the Anatomy of Action to Karen and asked her what it provoked for her. Karen spotted many aspects that she could immediately change in her relationship with Kay.

Karen shared that she had never explicitly articulated her cares to Kay—cares about their organization, client satisfaction and culture of performance that Karen wished to build.

Karen went on to share that there were several conversations that seemed to hang in the air, did not end in any clarity or actions. Kay would get upset with too many questions, would get emotional and report ill the next day. Karen would not broach those topics again fearing this kind of reaction.

Karen decided to share her care with Kay and enquire about Kay's care in return. She figured that there were far too many missing and incomplete conversations with Kay and they needed attending. She made a list of all her concerns. With respect and care, she tackled each of those conversations with Kay. Karen was direct, clear and said exactly what she needed to without allowing herself to be fazed by Kay's emotional responses. Where required, she allowed respite to Kay but picked up the conversation again allowing Kay to know that she wanted resolution.

She made it clear that she took care of what Kay cared about and gave her recognition at every possible occasion. She also held the same resolve in leaving no missing conversations between them. Karen found that in doing this, they could turn around the escalations from the client while Kay's team began to perform effectively. The team was also better integrated and aligned with the rest of the organization.

Santhya Vikram, founder of Yellow Train shares her story on care:

'We were moving out of our small Yellow Train school campus. It was the first campus where the school began. This campus was in one part of the city and we were now making plans of moving in another direction, right across the city as part of our expansion plans. Most of our parent community and all our teachers came from that locality where we were in, and in this move we were risking losing all our teachers and perhaps most of our parents. I was spending sleepless nights agonizing over it. Over one of the conversations with my team, I shared my angsts and came to terms with these struggles.

We had several ideation sessions and arrived at a plan that included several conversations with parents, building a new community of teachers and preparing for the new situation.

We decided to share what we care about—our care of continuity for parents and teachers, our care of keeping the community strong and intact, and the fact that we wish all our children could continue. The sensitivity with which the communication was made was central to the whole exercise. Sharing our 'care' was at the core of the messaging. The aspect of aligning our care with that of the parents and presenting the whole plan keeping their care at the centre of it, is what touched most parents. That has been one of my biggest learning in leading the school. No matter what the change, no matter what the hardship when you are sensitive to the other's care and can share it in the most authentic way along with your own care, people can see and experience what matters to you.

At the end of the year, not only did we create a new team and a new space we also had 80 per cent of our parents with us, most of who actually decided to relocate their homes near our new campus. Such was their commitment and love for our work with their children. Such was the result of aligning cares.

The above example is a powerful one that shows that when we bring our care into the conversation and share it, the unsurmountable seems possible. Our motivations, interests and purpose are revealed and this impacts the other.

How often are we keen to know why the other may participate in a task and deliver what we need? What drives them? In an organization, not understanding the other's care is like blindness. We disconnect ourselves from the other by thinking that the discussion we are having is just about a task or a project. People work for titles, for compensation and for reward. They also work because they are excited, find meaning in their work, experience growth and self-esteem, get opportunities to be part of a bigger exciting creation and many more such reasons.

Connecting with what the other cares about and supporting that process so they can achieve what they care about is a radical way of making a conversation and a relationship rich and powerful.

It is another way to align with each other to explore a shared care as we work together.[3]

In workshops I am often asked: Can there always be a shared care? Perhaps, but not always. At times we may not have a shared care, and exploration reveals that it is tough to align our cares. This is very revealing as it can inform us how we may take forward that relationship and what future we can create together or not create together. When there are no shared cares, a sustainable and rich partnership at work is a challenge. As leaders it allows us to make a choice of the relationships we wish to invest in and which we wish to let go.

Practice 1

- Identify what the missing conversations are at your workplace. Name the conversations you wish to have but don't have due to various reasons.

- Make a note of at least one conversation with a subordinate, a peer and a boss that you can have next week.

- To prepare for it, make a note of your care and what matters to you. Collect data that helps you call it out and substantiate what you say. Be clear with your intention of having that conversation.

[3] Bob Dunham has referred to this in his paper 'The Generative Foundations of Action in Organizations: Speaking and Listening' published in the *International Journal of Coaching in Organizations*, 2009.

- Converse with care and respect for the other. Use the points above to support you.

Understand that the purpose of a missing conversation isn't always resolution. It is to exercise your power as a leader to notice, call out and bring value to the environment you function in. It is about serving some care of yours. It is also about having the responsibility to take action for the sake of our cares. We grow our leadership and our confidence in these moments of practice.

Practice 2

Identify with whom you tend to have incomplete and ineffective conversations. We know we have ineffective conversations because we often have breakdowns and encounter things not working out repeatedly. Is it with a peer or a colleague or customer? Who do you see as authority?

Note what your hesitations are about. Here are a few possibilities that you may find:

- Not wanting to sound rude
- Not wanting to come across as difficult or sticky
- Not wanting to rock the conversation by bringing up what others have not raised
- Not wanting to show up as 'too smart'
- Not wanting to show up as a 'questioner'
- Not wanting to be disrespectful to their thinking
- Imagining that they must know what they are saying or want, so why speak?

Ask yourself how you could table your thoughts especially by connecting to their care on the task/project.

When you do that effectively how could it add value to the task, team or to the client?

When you begin to have complete and effective conversations how does it shift your public identity as a leader?

Practice 3

- Think of a colleague with whom you believe you do not share the greatest of equations. You seem to disagree or get into a rough spot at work.

- Note down what your care is in that project that you and your colleague contribute to.

- Why do you hold that care?

- How are your actions contributing to the care?

- How do you think your colleague's actions are probably challenging the wellness or workability of the project? Notice the 'probably'—it is important to hold this stance of reflection and not certainty.

- What data if any, could be useful to collect and share with your colleague?

- Should you have a 'shared care' discussion with your colleague, what could you share about your care with him/ her?

- What questions can you ask to understand what they care about and why?

- What questions, anecdotes, data can you be curious about in order to share and arrive at what is common in the cares that you both have?

From here you can begin to plan more conversations with this colleague so you arrive at agreements on how you and them/ team may function differently. All this is held within the container of the 'shared care' that has been discussed.

Reflect on what happens to teamwork, trust and your capacity to lead as you become a person who can have these conversations with others. Become aware of what new possibilities you now see merge.

You can apply the same set of reflections to a customer/client conversation too!

Chapter 7

BEING PRESENT

Presence includes several aspects—it means paying attention to ourselves, what arises within us as well as outside of us, and it feeds our capacity to communicate powerfully. It is a kind of 'knowing' which is connected to 'being present' in the here and now. Taisen Deshimaru, a Zen roshi says, 'We think with the whole body'.

A leader who is present extends a certain quality of inclusiveness. This could be during a meeting, at an event or even on a call with a customer who is miles away.

Being present expands our personal space. We then develop a capacity to feel and be sensitive to the environment around us. It is like having an active antenna.

Tara

Tara was the CEO of an organization that developed software. One of her clients was a start-up company with a product idea that Tara and her team were developing. The developers had finished 20 per cent of the work and were in a demo meeting with the client.

While Tara sat through the meeting quietly listening, she noticed that the client appeared comfortable—but something was amiss for her. She sensed that something in the direction of their work needed change but didn't know what.

Her inner self sensed her own discomfort and was aware of the clients' body language. They appeared comfortable but perhaps, they too felt like something was missing.

It was as though she had an antenna that sensed inwards and another that sensed outwards, tapping into the field of the other as well as the energy in the room. She expressed her thoughts to the client. She began asking them questions and boldly suggested to the client—'Never mind the 20 per cent work. Let's put this aside and go back to the drawing board'. She asked if the client was willing to go back to the fundamentals of the product concerned, and think of fresh ideas. Her invitation to them was to think through this together.

A lot changed on that project and the client decided to take a new direction. This was all because one person was 'switched on' or present through that meeting. Tara was not scared of listening to the broadcast within herself and tune into the broadcast from the environment, nor did she hesitate to communicate this broadcast. This ability to be present changed both Tara's and her client's work for the better.

Presence Is about Cultivating an Openness to What Is

Presence is expressed as a mindful and connected interest in the other by carrying openness into a discussion without being afraid of what could come up.

The appraisal meeting

Performance evaluation can be a stressful time in most organizations. Tara was sitting in on an appraisal discussion with an employee and his manager. The employee seemed concerned about the rating that his manager had given him but wasn't saying much. He had a sullen, quiet look while the manager kept sharing data as to why he had rated the employee in such a manner.

Tara's antenna was active. She could sense something was 'cooking' within the employee. She saw through the silence. As if her antenna had the capacity to dip into the other and know that all was not well, Tara said to the employee: 'I've been listening to your manager speak all this while. I sense something is not agreeable to you in this discussion. Would you like to tell us what the issue is? Any discomfort with this process?'

It was as though the gates had opened with that one question. The employee shared his concerns, the breakdowns in their team, why he thought the data that the manager had shared was not complete and many other finer details.

The appraisal meeting could have ended with a disgruntled employee. Instead, it ended with an employee expressing his vulnerability, a CEO and a manager receiving much needed data they didn't have and a trust was established between the three parties involved.

The employee expressed: 'It feels good to know that I can be heard here'.

Tara's question invited a certain vulnerability in the employee which she held with respect and genuine interest. Her presence was not about protecting herself or the manager. Instead, it was about allowing herself to be transparent and understanding.

Mindful interest is about holding an attitude that says 'I want to work better with you'.

Being present is a practice and can be learnt. In a world abuzz with activity, technology and noise, teaching ourselves to look within ourselves is vital. It holds the power to transform ourselves, stay humane and connected to others.

Presence is one of the cornerstones of leadership, one that gives us the capacity to use our antenna to sense and express ourselves in ways that are open, productive and focussed on the other. Through this openness we understand others cares and what ideas would best support them.

Presence is not knowledge or going into one's head in order to understand and think. Presence is mind plus body and sensing into self and a situation. It is both skill and common sense, all experienced in our body through a deep inner listening. When we are present and open to another we pick up signals in the environment as well as internal intuitive signals too.

'Academic Knowledge is an intellectual understanding: it fills the head with information. This has its place in certain domains, but in the domain of leadership it is not always relevant. Embodied knowledge on the other hand, is the skill to act appropriately at the appropriate time. It is immediate, available and responsive', Richard Strozzi-Heckler says this in his book *Leadership Dojo*. (1)

Being present in the way Tara was, allows us to be responsive to the other with a heightened state of problem solving, while also keeping the connection with the other intact.

Three significant things Tara did: In both the situations Tara sensed herself and the other first. She was fully aware of what was being said and what was not said. She did this with her *expansive presence*.

Open connected listening is what she practised next. She brought openness, respect and value for the self and the other. This helped her add value to the relational space between her and the other.

Lastly she *'gave voice'* to her inner broadcast with clarity and vulnerability while inviting the other to express and participate. All this she did with no fear, defensiveness or aggression.

Tara practised a fundamental form of presence called 'Centering'— a practice of tuning into the inner self, our thoughts, emotions and body sensations. It is also about tuning into the external environment using our senses.

'If your learning isn't in your body', asks Peter Senge, 'then where is it?' (2)

Many of us believe that 'sensing' and 'thinking' happens in our mind or inside our heads. Growing evidence suggests that thinking also happens in the physicality of our body. The body does this thinking through the senses with which it experiences the world and takes in stimuli. Within us are myriad of sensations, images, emotions and stories all contained in our 'body'. We need to begin listening and developing inner ears so we are sensing within the self as well as outside of ourselves.

The believability of someone's message is influenced 7 per cent by content, 38 per cent by voice tone and 55 per cent by body language. (3) Many of us can recall a time when we went ahead with a plan simply because we 'felt' like we could trust the other. This trust was more a sense we had of the other person and not necessarily a data-driven decision. This means that there probably was something in the person's demeanour—how they spoke, moved, sat or made eye contact. Perhaps, that influenced us to trust them and feel safe in going ahead. Presence is therefore a kind of vocabulary with which we communicate to others that: 'I can be trusted' or 'I am okay with you'. (1)

I really wish to understand you

Vania was a senior leader who was promoted to head a business group of 800 people.

She was very performance driven and strived to be at the top of her game for herself. She had told me that being good at whatever she did was her strategy for success. She had been at the top of her class from her school days! She wore a look of a stressed out, uptight person in action all the time and was most times in a hurry to arrive some place. A core area of her coaching need was developing her leadership presence. This was because she now needed to build trust not just with her new team but also with stakeholders in other geographies.

As her coach, she invited me to sit in on her meeting with her team making it explicit that this was part of her own coaching agenda and not about the team. During the meeting, I saw her tell her team member, 'I really wish to understand what you mean by that' and while she said that I noticed her body. She was stiff, there was no smile, her eyes had a hard gaze and the tone was stiff too.

I wondered what that same conversation may have been like had she sat in an 'easy' posture, had a relaxed face, spoken slowly and used a warm tone. The words may be the same but the flavour of the interaction would be transformed. I don't think Vania was aware of how she came across to others. Seeing her connect in this way throughout the meeting enabled me to see why her team may not trust her yet, although she was trying so hard. Due to her uptight energy, her team probably felt the strain in her communication and her presence.

Stress and how it knocks out 'presence'

I grew up in a home that placed a premium on doing well, being effective and efficient, as well as aiming high. I also grew up in Mumbai—a city where life is fast-paced and stressful. From a young age my body learnt to be tensed. My stomach was in a permanent clench—a clench that held this message: 'I need to do more, I need to move faster... I need to be better'.

When I began to learn presence practices, it was like learning a technique to relax this clench. I learnt to relax all of my body. I became sensitive to when and how the clench began forming in my body—almost always in response to threat, stress or fear.

Learning to be mindful helped me see my habitual clenching pattern. My body had learnt and practised this clenching for long. The clench always brought up my personal history.

I realized that I can never do away with stressful situations altogether. Things will not work the way I wish and that is a reality of life. With practice I learnt to recognize what the clench felt like in my body and the triggers in the environment. This awareness allowed me to anticipate when I may lose balance and feel tense again. With mindfulness I learnt to manage those moments and shift from the place of 'clench', by telling myself that a relaxed mind and body will perform better.

Centring as a Somatic Practice for Presence

I had already been practicing 'presence'-based meditations for a while. I heard the word 'Centring'[1] first in the context of training with the Institute of Generative leadership, United States.

[1] I learnt this from Bob Dunham in the Coaching Excellence in Organizations programme organized by the Institute for Generative Leadership, USA. Bob attributes this to Richard Strozzi-Heckler of the Strozzi Institute.

Centring is the process of collecting ourselves—Richard Strozzi

I have developed my own version of Centring from the various teachers I have learnt it from and I now introduce it to leaders as a way to keep our balance in a pressured environment. It helps keep us dignified during conflict. When we know our centre and are balanced, we can move any way we want from a place of choice. We move from a place of choice, not reaction.

When in conflicted or stressful situations, some of us tighten or contract our body. That is the natural fear-based response of our body. I was recently at an Alexander Technique special lesson and the teacher told me that most of us will measure an inch lesser by evening when compared to the morning, as our spine would be compressed owing to the stresses of our day! It explained to me why many of us tend to complain of neck and back problems developed out of stress reactions.

Centre is not a permanent static place. It is a place we move out of and become off-centre, and then comes the moment where we notice that we are off-centre. From that moment comes choice to reorient and make a movement back to centre. It is a process that we mindfully attend to.

Your deepest presence is in every small contracting and expanding, the two as beautifully balanced and coordinated as birdwings.—Rumi

Centring helps us find balance by becoming aware of our internal states while continually also sensing external environment through our senses. Andy Bryner and Dawna Markova in describe Centring as: '...a process by which you integrate the habitually fragmented aspects of yourself-body, mind, spirit, heart, power and common sense-back into their natural state of integrity. (4) Practically, this results in an increased awareness of the moment and your presence in it. Rather than becoming a victim to whom things are happening, you become an active agent of your life'.

Centring also helps us regulate our emotions and become deeply aware of them.

Many of us do not recognize our emotional states at all. We don't always know the difference between fear, rage, anger, disappointment or the many minute emotional states we experience in the day. Many of us have practised a specific reactive response to a situation and that reaction often does not help us solve problems effectively. At times these practiced reactive patterns influence us to say and do things that are not dignified or mature. The loss is the impact it has on our public identity, our self-esteem and our relationships.

Being emotionally aware serves us well as emotions are an important component of good decision-making. Knowing our emotional state allows us to make a choice of what we wish to do and why. It prompts us to be more mindful in our actions.

Dull anxiety all day

Vania and I had a coaching conversation a few months after I had been an observer at her team meeting. She had begun the practice of Centring and she shared that her capacity for observation of her emotional states had increased tremendously.

She was aware that she often experienced a fear of disagreement during her team meetings. She noticed that the emotion she experienced throughout the day was what she termed a 'dull anxiety'. The same team members had been her peers until recently and she was afraid of their challenge in meetings. This fear made her body rigid, at times her jaw would feel clenched, and her breath was shallow.

Becoming aware of her fear allowed her to take a deep breath and relax to centre herself. From that centred place, she became aware that she can smile more, soften her tone to sound easy rather than anxious or overwhelmed. She began taking time off in the day to do centring practice because the pauses helped her collect herself and decide how to move ahead. She shared that she was less reactive and was able to respond to situations in a direct but non-confrontational manner. She began feeling better about her capacity to lead as she felt more confident through the day rather than anxious all the time.

Being present is like your GPS.
Pay attention and it informs you
how to navigate.

Centring as Clarifying Our Thought Process

Imagine a tall glass of water. If you pour water into it, put in some gravel and begin to swirl it around with a spoon, what do you think that glass will look like? A swirling brown mixture, perhaps with small and big pieces of gravel all turning around with the water. When one is overwhelmed or confused, our mind resembles this swirling brown glass of water. We experience myriad thoughts all at the same time and our mind feels murky and disturbed like the swirling water.

Imagine now that you stop stirring and allow the glass to 'just be'. What do you imagine we will notice? The gravel settles, there is more clearness to the water, a stillness in which you can see through the glass with clarity and begin to notice in detail the nature and quality of the gravel inside. Centring as a practice allows us to do just this with our mind.

By observing our thoughts, we are able to see clearly the nature of our thoughts and what occupies our mind at the moment. Seeing what we are occupied with is so useful as it allows us to attend to it or allows us to put it away for the time being, while being present to where we are right now. It is a practice to be in the now and learn to have an undisturbed mind. A fully present mind and body together are able to connect with those around, and see the concerns in that moment. We are able to attend to that which needs attention. Settling the mind allows us to see priorities more clearly. It allows us to sort out data, see patterns and respond with energy or flexibility, firmness or even compassion, whatever the situation may call for.

I stayed calm

Seema was in one of the one-year women leadership courses. At the start of the programme, she shared about this male colleague who was technical, smart and often overwhelmed her with technical details she didn't always follow. Despite being in the technical stream, she felt she was not good enough because she assessed herself as less competent and knowledgeable than him. She had noticed that as a way of covering up her insecurity, she often got aggressive with him or at times felt very passive and quiet, thinking she wasn't good enough. Her extreme behaviours confused this colleague and the relationship was strained.

She had been practising centring for a bit and during one of the workshops shared that the previous week she was face to face with this smart colleague again. She shared, 'I stayed centred and refused to go to either of the extremes. I could notice that the triggers were there, but I felt calm. I noticed that I was feeling insecure and yet I did not allow myself to be aggressive. It was a comfortable conversation and I could keep my connection to my colleague instead of feeling detached or upset'. Being in a comfortable relationship with the colleague was important for her and she was happy that centering supported this shift in her.

I invite you to build these presence practices into your day. Allow this new way of listening and sensing to support you in navigating tricky situations and relationships.

Practice 1

Pick a chair with an armrest. In the chair sit with your back erect, but not rigid. Your head rests on your spine. Be aware that your head is not leaning to the right or the left. It just sits easy on your spine. Have your feet flat on the ground and arms resting on the arm rest or in your lap in an open posture, palms facing up or down.

Now bring your focus to how your body feels in the chair. Become aware of how the back of the chair supports you and how the seat of the chair supports your leg. Notice the weight of your body on your buttocks, the muscles and bones you use to sit.

Bring your focus now to your breath, breathe in and breathe out. Do not make any effort, just allow your natural breathing. Allow your breath to fall into your belly as you breathe in and out. Belly breathe for another minute or so.

Bring your focus now to your body. If you feel any tightness in any part of your body, just gently move that part or do a small stretch to allow it to relax. Imagine your breath is flowing into those tight muscles allowing them to relax.

We are attempting to observe and become acutely aware of all sensations as we sit. Tiny and gross sensations.

Once again notice your breath. It has slowed down.

Allow 3–4 minutes to pass and slowly open your eyes. Become aware of the surroundings and the space you sit in. Just notice.

Practice 2

This practice is about acutely experiencing our senses, beginning to listen, sensing the internal and the external, and to toggle between the two a few times. It takes about 10 minutes and I recommend doing this a minimum of once a day as a practice.

Find a comfortable chair with armrests or a sofa where you may fold your feet and sit.

If you are in a chair sit with feet reaching the ground, keep your feet flat on the ground. Keep your spine erect and head placed right on top of the spine. The head is not bending to the right or left. You are erect but not rigid.

Bring your attention to your breath, your natural breath going in and out. Allow yourself to belly breathe naturally.

Bring your attention now to the smells, sounds and tastes you can access. Including awareness on your skin, surface of temperature and textures. Acutely experience your senses.

Bring your attention to your body as you check for any sensations, itch, pain or tightness anywhere in your body. Breathe and allow that part to relax. If it is a sensation, just notice it.

Bring your attention now to your thoughts, observing them streaming in and leaving like guests to your home! No need to push them away or do anything. Just observe them. Know what they are about.

Come back to observing the breath.

Come back to observing the senses and what they pick up externally.

Come back to the body sensations and back to the thoughts.

Repeat this internal and external process a few times.

Notice how the breath has slowed down.

Notice how clearly you can see your thoughts

Notice the body.

A centred space.[2]

---

[2] The full practice version of this can be downloaded at www.physis.co.in

References

1. Strozzi-Heckler Richard. *The leadership dojo: Build your foundation as an exemplary leader*. Berkely, CA: Frog Books, 2007.

2. Senge Peter. *The fifth discipline fieldbook*. New York, NY: Currency/Doubleday, 1994.

3. Mehrabian Albert. *Silent messages: Implicit communication of emotions and attitudes*. 2nd ed. Florence, KY: Wadsworth, 1981.

4. Bryner Andy and Markova Dawna. *An unused intelligence*. Berkeley, CA: Conari Press, 1996.

THE FIVE-FINGER SOLUTION

In all the chapters so far we have looked at the observer that we are and the importance of becoming aware of our inner language or inner chatter. We've begun to notice that within our observer lies our personal history as well as the many assessments that we hold about ourselves and others, and from there comes a certain set of actions and results.

We've also looked at our personal GREENs connected with fuelling our actions and dreams, and moving beyond the adaptive patterns we may have unconsciously adopted.

All of these are at different places in the journey of stepping into ourselves, and stepping out from our shadows and limiting actions as well as thought patterns.

Now we're going to look at stepping up tools.

Language is a way of defining a new identity for ourselves and others. It is a way of creating and seeing new possibilities as language creates a new observer in us.

'Generative language has the power to create new futures, to craft vision and to eliminate the blinders that are preventing people from seeing possibilities'. (1) Fernando Flores synthesized the work of

Martin Heidegger and John Searle's theory of speech acts to produce a new understanding of language and communication.[1] He said that in language we shift the future through the commitments we make, in the way we listen to and ask for commitments too.

A big part of what we do in organizations is coordinating action with others. We're getting things done in a way that is meaningful and satisfying for us and for others. It is taking care of some significant care of ours and of others.

The Five-Finger Solution

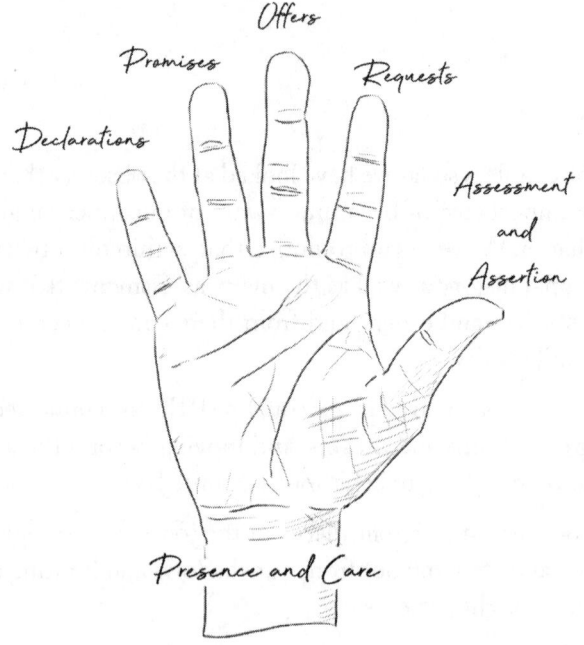

Five-Finger Solution

[1] Bob Dunham has referred to this in his paper 'The Generative Foundations of Action in Organizations: Speaking and Listening' published in the *International Journal of Coaching in Organizations*, 2009. Many of Flores ideas can be found in a book he authored with Charles Spinoza and Hubert Dreyfus, *Disclosing New Worlds*. John Searle wrote *Speech Acts and the Expression of Meaning* and Fernando Flores synthesized some of these ideas with ideas from Martin Heidegger and biologist Humberto Maturana.

Each of our fingers can be attributed with a language action or a 'speech act'. When we can attend to each of those language actions, we can find ways to get unstuck from where we are. Most often, the solution to any situation, conflict, stuckness and ambiguity lies in one of these five aspects.

These speech acts are also that which advance us towards our goals, allow us to open possibilities for self and others, and support us in taking our biggest gifts to the world!

They practically inform us of the next conversation we need to have. They help us move towards the next step.

The base of these five fingers is presence and care. We have already established that being present to our self, others and the environment informs us—so we choose our next steps. Being present allows us to use our inner ears to listen to the chatter inside of us and to listen to the ideas and wisdom that are arising within. Our listening of the external world allows us to read our environment, sense the energy behind spoken words and listen to the verbal and non-verbal language of those around us.

Our care establishes our direction and energy for our actions. It connects with that which has meaning and motivation for ourselves and which has value for the other.

The five language actions are:

- Assessments and assertions
- Requests
- Offers
- Promises
- Declarations

Assessments and assertions are one of the first language actions to consider. These language actions need to be checked out upfront as they reveal to us very early on the observer that we are. Once we have a glimpse into our assessments and find a way to ground them, and know our assertions in a given context, they inform what our next step could be. Evaluating our assessments in themselves changes our lens to problem solving and actions.

Assessments and assertions, requests, offers, promises and declarations are other speech acts and they have a RED zone that we may fall into. When we fall into those REDs, we get stuck, the GREENs in each of them allow us to get unstuck and through language we can generate effective action in us and others.

The five-finger solution operationalizes the Adult ego state by providing clarity as to what our next move in a conversation needs to be. The next move is for attending to a relationship, a task or a problem that needs solving or a possibility we wish to open for ourselves.

Five Fingers and Our Public Identity

Why is managing our public identity of significance? Notice your responses to these situations.

- Imagine a person who speaks with assumptions and uses very little data.

- Imagine a person who lives with many negative assumptions of self and others. How do they come across to others?

- Imagine needing a favour or a task done from others but asking it with tremendous obligation or not asking at all.

- Imagine a person making commitments of doing a task but forever procrastinating.

- Imagine someone gave you a commitment but slipped up and forgot about it.

- Imagine a person with great potential and strengths but always wanting to play safe.

I imagine that your response to the above situations may have any of these: 'not very impressive'; 'can't count on this person'; 'hurt at being treated so shabbily'; 'not a potent or powerful individual'.

Most of us are impressed by individuals who act with care, confidence and integrity. These are essential aspects of a public identity of a leader. Taking charge of our public identity and building it so we show up in a particular way to others is our responsibility. Our public identity needs managing! Managing it by no means manipulation. Instead, I mean manage it by paying attention to it for the sake of building trust and connection with others. Trust and connection are fundamental to leading.

Building public identity is about care.
Are you connected to what you care about?
Are your energy and actions backing your care?
Are you showing others what you care about?
Are you in conversations connected to your care?

A leader who functions in this way shows up differently to others. We primarily show up as aligned with our actions and where we wish to invest time and energy. We change how we use time and conversations. We alter in others eyes, their understanding of our actions and why we take a particular stance. We show up as an individual who is willing to do what it takes to take care of our care. We make commitments responsibly and have the same attitude to commitments others make to us. We are willing to play bigger for the sake of what we care about.

This kind of leading has an energetic quality to it and a quality of conviction that all of us wish to be associated with. We get noticed as effective and potent. We are wanted in committees and work groups for the value in our thinking and weight of our words. We are seen as value adding due to the offers we shape. We are looked up to for the promises we keep. We are associated with for the bigger games we play in the world and who we play with!

The five finger actions allow us to examine ourselves and build this kind of public identity as leaders.

Practice 1

- Reflect on how you are showing up as a leader in your organization?
- Have you been shaping your public identity?
- How has your care been preset in your actions, conversations and what you showcase?
- What can you begin doing differently so you design your public identity?

Reference

1. Zaffron Steve and Logn Dave. *The three laws of performance: Rewriting the future of your organization and your life.* San Francisco, CA: Jossey-Bass/Wiley/Times Group Books, 2009.

Chapter 9

ASSESSMENTS AND ASSERTIONS

In one of my courses I had a participant say: 'I cannot have meaningless conversations with strangers. I am not a networking kind of person. Going to events where I exchange business cards and introduce myself to umpteen numbers of people does not appeal to me.

In another group coaching call a lady said: 'I am a shy person, I cannot stand up and make presentations easily. But I am better at interacting one to one with people'.

In a workshop on communication I had a participant say: 'I can think of at least one colleague with whom none of what you are saying will apply. He is manipulative, slimy and looks for every opportunity to get me down. In fact, I think most of his team also functions like that—all out to get people and prove others wrong. Actually come to think of it, the entire sales team has this attitude. I think their work makes them pushy and manipulative'.

A workshop participant once shared: 'In the last year, I have stopped laughing loud and carry myself quietly because my leader gave me feedback that it is very unbecoming for me to be so loud'.

Is it not interesting that we speak of ourselves and others with such clarity, certainty and finality? Each of these people believed deeply in what they were saying.

I am very certain about what I know, what I don't know, who I am, what I can do, what I can't do, I'm this kind of person, I am that kind of person....We speak of it with great certainty. This certainty is held like a truth. Some of these certainties are about ourselves, who we are. Some of the certainties are about who others are and some are about how situations are.

What each of these individuals expressed is what is called 'an assessment'. Assessments are part of your observer's lens.

Where are these 'certainties' coming from? Answering this question can build our personal awareness and help understand these statements better.

The observer that I am holds these assessments. Have you considered 'How come I have this thought?'; 'Where has it come from?'; 'Where have I learnt this?'; 'Where have I taken this lens from?'

'I must strive for perfection…that's the way to be successful'.
'Everyone is better than me'.
'This particular task is very tough. I can't manage it'.
'People who are like that can manage this task. Not me'.
'People from sales teams only know to be pushy and manipulative'.
'Customers cannot be questioned'.

All these statements are good examples of assessments because there is a particular observer that holds these assessments. If you ask a different observer, they may not have the same statements. We hold these as truths and those truths begin to guide what we do in the world with ourselves and with others.

Where do these truths come from? One obvious source is culture. A lot of 'truths' that we hold comes from culture. Whether it is about what good women are or who a good mother is. Who is a good woman leader and what her ideal behaviour is.

Another major source of these truths is those that we get from our families. These are told to us constantly and reinforced in many ways or we just observe what our family follows and we hold the same as truths.

Sometimes these truths come from people of authority who tell us early on in life what we should or should not believe. As they are people of authority, they have some sway over us. We adopt their 'truth'.

Sometimes we fail to notice where we get these truths from and how we hold these assessments. It is as though we create a story and then we forget we have the story. However, unknown to us the story guides what we do and will not do.

Fish do not know they live in water. We are unaware of our assessments on self, others and situations just like fish are unaware of water around them.

Assessments on money

I was coaching a leader of an organization that worked for children's education. The organization did some fabulous work in this field and had become quite successful. But they ran into financial challenges as the organization needed to make some significant decisions on growth and expansion. Resources and funds needed to be organized and allocated to these growth plans.

In my coaching conversations with the leader, her vision for the project, deep conviction and competence in the field of education became evident and shined through whatever she spoke. Her plans for what she wanted to accomplish with the children and her team were impressive. However, I noticed that she did not concern herself with financial issues even though she was the CEO. There were family members who took care of those issues. One of her goals for the year was to take full charge of being CEO, including being in charge of the financials. Our conversations revealed that she was a particular kind of observer of finances and money. Informing her observer were several assessments: 'Money is just a means to the end'; 'If one holds good intention, then support and help will just appear'; 'I am here to make the lives of children change and that is all that concerns me'; '"I am not the kind of person who will get too concerned about resources and somehow it will get taken care of'. Such assessments limited her vision and field of action. It was a story that she had told herself and unconsciously, that story shaped who she became. She lived in that story so much that she didn't notice it existed. Remember the fish and the water?

The story governed her actions. In staying away from matters of finance and related decisions in her organization, she was staying away from some significant aspects of her leadership role. As the CEO, she needed to be responsible for expansion plans, managing risk—including financial and growing her team capability. All of this required her to focus on the financials. She hadn't considered this aspect at all! She revealed that she was brought up in a family that believed in 'Simple living, high thinking'; 'Money is not important'; 'Education is in itself a worthy goal and interest in money should not corrupt it'.

We discussed that she had a work experience of 12 years, that she knew from feedback that she had specific strengths and talents, and that she had been successful in her previous assignments. She had the necessary educational qualifications and competence to back her in her new project. Above all she had a strong care.

The work this leader needed to do was to learn to marry her lofty goals with good skills in financial appreciation and planning.

When she began seeing the story and how it dictated her behaviour, she felt compelled to update her story. She decided that as a leader she needs to update her story for effective action to happen. The observer in her decided that she is ready and good enough to take on this challenge. She made herself self sufficient in this area so she could take over financial aspects of her organization and actively participate as a full-fledged CEO within that year.

Assertions and Assessments

'This room is 300 sq. ft.' is an assertion because it is fact based.

'Andrea is strong and a good leader' is an assessment.

'The book weighs 4 kilos' is an assertion and the 'The book is heavy' is an assessment. We have attached qualities to the book. Assessments are not fact based.

Assertions are claims or facts and assessments are opinions or judgements, subjective statements. Assertions are about the thing that is being observed but assessments belong to the observer. (1)

In a meeting assertions reveal something about the object or subject being observed—'There are 10 people in the meeting and Rahul sits next to Andrea'.

When I remark in a judgmental way: 'Rahul did not wish Veena good morning today'. I am making an assessment. Assessments reveal much more about the observer and the standards of the observer. This means that I expected Rahul to wish her 'Good morning', but when he didn't, I noticed it. The observer in us has a particular standard of what is okay and what is not okay and the assessments arise from there. When the school leader in the aforementioned example said 'Money is just a means', it revealed the kind of observer she was about money but also about what she thought was the role of a leader vis a vis managing funds.

Assertions have to do with the past and the present, while assessments have everything to do with the future. (1) For example, if we look at assertions: 'In yesterday's meeting, Joel came late by 30 minutes', it is a statement describing what happened. Or 'In today's meeting Joel has come 30 minutes late', it describes what is happening.

But the assessment I make about Joel is: 'Joel is unreliable'. This is about the future as it influences how I will be with Joel, what I will rely on him for etc. Similarly, the school leader's assessments on money was all about the future as it predisposed her to act in a certain manner in her present and future, which was to stay distant on monetary issues.

Lastly, assertions are about how things truly are. Assessments are about what you make of it. (1) 'The grass outside is brown' is an assertion. You look at it and see it is brown. 'Brown grass is unappealing' is an assessment and it is what I make of what the grass is. The school leader was making lack of fiscal knowledge and being in charge as a non-issue that didn't matter to the organization. It is what she made of the issue. There was no fact in it.

Why Is Examining Our Assessments Important?

When we look at problem solving or when we look at changing ourselves or a situation, it is very useful to begin to understand 'What assessments do I hold about—myself, the other and the situation?' This is a vital reflection I invite you to make.

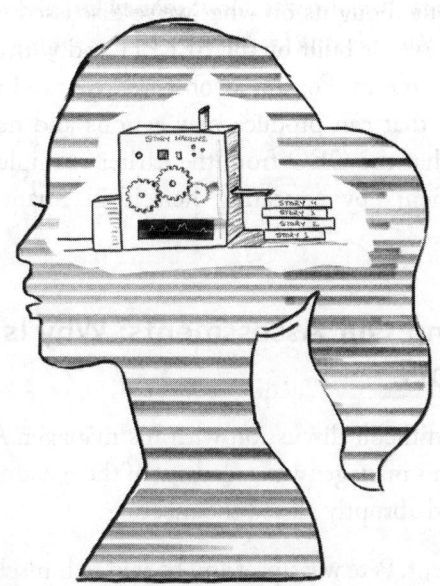

We are assessment machines—we churn out several stories and we forget that we made them.
Unexamined assessments can limit how we generate outcomes for self and others.

These assessments are going to enable you to act in a particular way, not take any action at all or take ineffective action. Identifying assessments is one of the key aspects to observe so that we can make shifts in who we are and how we act.

The other reason why examining assessments is vital is because the assessments we make influence how we are with others. Our assessments open or close possibilities with others. If we have a favourable assessment toward another, that is great as it keep possibilities open with the other. On the other hand if we have negative assessments about the other, it often closes possibilities with another as we often act according to our assessments.

To collect our thoughts on what we've discussed so far, we know that an observer is built by the SELPH and within that we have tons of assessments. For a new observer, we need newer, updated assessments that can produce new actions and new results. This is exactly what the CEO from the earlier example did—updated her assessments by educating herself in finances and taking new actions.

Grounding Our Assessments: Why Is This Important?

Pete had a difficult discussion with his manager. As the meeting continued, his manager was called out of the meeting. The manager returned and abruptly closed the meeting.

An assessment: Pete was upset and he said to himself: 'My manager doesn't care for what I was discussing. Everything else seems more important'.

Assertion: The manager was called out of the meeting. He closed the meeting and left (we don't know why).

Pete spoke to Priya about escalating an issue to their manager. Priya refused and said she did not wish to take it up at that time and that she needed to give it some thought. Pete was very upset and walked off.

Assessment: Pete concluded: 'Priya has no spine. When it comes to doing what is important, she backs of'.

Assertion: Priya refused to escalate the issue now. She asked for time to think about it.

Events like this transpire continuously at work. With each assessment, Pete was reaching a place of conclusion about a person. This place of conclusion that he reached changed how he behaved with Priya. He also built a predisposed attitude towards his manager.

My grounding story

A seed of an idea of developing an online course and forum for professional women had been sowed in me. However, I made no progress beyond the level of thought. I was unhappy with myself for not taking any action on it and decided to talk to a colleague, who is also a leadership coach. As we spoke I heard myself for the first time, revealing my hesitations: 'I don't understand anything about this line of work'; 'I have never ever attended an online course myself so I cannot set one up'; 'I have no experience with this medium so why take risks in doing something you know nothing about?'; 'No one is doing it here in India so maybe it is not an idea that will fly'. These were all assessments I had made about myself and the situation. Notice how these assessments closed up possibilities for me. Staying with these ideas kept me stuck. I did not seek to clarify; I did not seek to explore options. In fact it kept me away from relevant action and put me in a mood of frustration because I wanted to do something about the issue and wasn't doing it. I was in one of my REDS which was lot of thinking and no action!

My colleague was patient and supportive in hearing me out. He reflected on all my assessments and mirrored them back to me in a new way. I could look at them with new eyes.

He helped me ground my assessments with his powerful questions and examples:

'Who said you need to experience something in order to do it?'

'What strengths and gifts do you have that you can carry powerfully into a project like this?'

'No one has offered it in your market yet. This means that it is a great opportunity to break in and make a difference'

'If you don't have personal expertise, do you know others in a different community who may help educate you and advise you?'

'What small steps can you take to manage your risk in this project rather than not start because you are anxious?'

These questions were like a torchlight in a dark room. The light was coming from a powerful new observer that my colleague was. His observer did not hold any of the assessments that I did. He held up for me a picture of endless possibilities. I realized that my assessments were holding me back and they needed these 'grounding questions' that opened up a new set of actions. I also uncovered some assertions that were important for me to note, namely:

I had over 20 years' experience in personal transformation work.

I have my training as a therapist, trainer supervisor and an ICF credentialed coach.

I belong in multiple communities of support and expertise.

I had completed conversations with several diversity represen-tatives within organizations who indicated that such a product would be valuable. I had data.

I am grateful to have access to such powerful tools of thought. At every stage, I have the grounding questions that help me check my assessments and know the assertions that matter.

The result of this conversation was that I went ahead with small steps, made a plan and got advisors on board with my project. I gave myself some time to gain small experiences as a learner. I created a network of support and put a team together. In 10 months, I launched Step Up—a four-month online course for women in leadership.

It is natural to make assessments. We will never reach a state of not having assessments. In fact, sometimes people ask: 'Can we only function with assertions?' No, we can't as sometimes as leaders we also function in spaces of the unknown—where we do not have much access to data. Yet, we need to move forward by making assessments.

In fact, I think assessments have, at the heart of them, a need to keep us safe and protect us. From a young age, we have practised protecting ourselves from scary, embarrassing or anxiety-provoking situations and sometimes, our assessments keep us safe as we do not step out of our comfort. It is our blindness that we don't realize we are constantly making these assessments and we keep interpreting them to be the truth.

When we assess ourselves to be shy, cannot manage some task, scared to try, we will fail etc., it is the young part in us that aspires to keep us safe from failing or showing up shabby or incompetent.

When we hold an assessment that 'others will not understand'; 'others are manipulative'; 'the world is harsh place', it is again a protective mechanism so we stop ourselves from moving toward the other for the sake of protection from hurt or harm.

Once we recognize that assessments were taken on for this sake of keeping ourselves safe and unhurt, we can bring ourselves to examine our assessments for their relevance and reality. Relevance and reality are both significant as we are no longer the same young self we once were. We have abilities, capacity for thought and action, ability to take care of ourselves, life experiences of ours and others to borrow from! Acknowledging this reality is important. Our Adult ego state is a super ally for reality checking.

I cannot intervene

I was coaching a woman leader Suhita who was next in line to the HR head. In her role, she did projects with the HR head as also with some of the business heads because in some projects that she led, business heads were stakeholders too. She claimed that she wasn't getting ahead as the HR head and some business leaders were at loggerheads with each other and so work was getting stalled. She seemed very confused and lost with how to move ahead. Each one told her their side of the story in private and she said: 'I feel like I am a ping pong ball. Sometimes on her side and sometimes on his'. She held assessments such as: 'They are really senior folk so I can't get into their games'; 'It does not look appropriate for me to speak up and call out their conflict'; 'It is not my place to speak up as it may have consequences for me'; 'Their equation is too messy'.

In coaching she began noticing the observer she was and realized that these assessments held an influence from an old place in her life. As a young person she could not handle her parents in conflict. When they argued or became loud, she would go away to another room to keep away from the noise and the bad mood. It kept her safe.

Through coaching she realized that these assessments were an old strategy for safety and that she had many strengths to combat the situation now. Another way to understand it is that she began to understand her Child state and began to see the full realities of her Adult state. In her Adult state, the new observer saw her strengths, abilities and resources so she could have this conversation with one of the seniors or both. She decided to call a meeting to address this rather than avoid it.

How to Ground Assessments?

'Grounding assessments' is a way for us to have more clarity and objectivity in our thinking and action. We do this by checking out our assessments and checking for the validity of our thought. (1)

- **When we talk about grounding, we must first listen to our assessment or our inner chatter.** Listen inside. What am I saying about this thing/person? What am I saying about myself? What am I saying about this situation?

- **'What is the reason am making this assessment?'** Why am I assessing that he is like this, or she is like this? For what purpose? Why is it important for me?

- **'In what domain am I making this assessment?** The assessment could be: 'Priya is unreliable', but in what domain? Priya may be not good in accounting but she may be great at handling events. If someone is unreliable in one domain, it doesn't mean that they cannot function well in another domain. Often we generalize and carry forward our assessments in such a way that they almost entirely colour our view of the individual.

- **'What is the standard that I'm using for making these assessments?'** Why am I using these standards? Is this standard relevant here? Am I willing to make do with another standard—maybe a higher or lower standard?

- **'What facts do I have to support the assessment I have made? What assertions can I make in this situation?'** What facts do I have that my manager does not like me? What facts do I have that says that my manager makes other things more important than me? What data do I have that supports my assessment that Priya is unreliable in managing this event?

- **'Is there a mood or an emotion connected to this assessment?'** Is there a scare or an anxiety or another emotion? How is it helping me? How is it stopping me?

These are a set of reflective or grounding questions that begin to reveal the observer we are.

The above grounding questions are a starter set. You can see in my grounding story that the colleague used many more 'reality check' questions to enable my new observer.

For Suhita I had to use many of these questions including the question on emotion and what shaped these assessments from her past. Of course, as a coach I could use a bigger range of these questions as I had a mandate to support her development.

As colleagues we cannot use a set a questions that delve into a team member or individual's past or personal life as that is a boundary we cannot cross and it is beyond our role as a colleague. However, all the above grounding questions are available to use as we support others in questioning their assessments and they can be applied to ourselves too so we do a good 'reality check'.

The grounding questions allow us to see a situation or person anew. They allow us to explore more options and open possibilities. Creating new possibilities and expanding options is one of the many actions that leaders to do. We don't always have a choice of teams we work with, colleagues we lead or a customer we partner with. It is easy to fall into assessments that limit us and hold on to them, but they do not help. Grounding our assessments helps us work with others in a new and different way than was possible before. By this I do not mean all caution is thrown to the wind. Through grounding we can take small steps to build trust or begin a small conversation to resolve the difficulty with people. We can explore a more effective way of connection and team work when we do not take our story as the 'absolute truth' and are willing to question it.

Grounding assessments gives us back our 'agency' to do what is important to take care of what we care about. Our agency includes our strengths, resources and inner wisdom that we forget to access but are always present within us.

Grounding assessments gives us back our 'agency' to do what is important to take care of what we care about. It allows us to see people and situations with fresh eyes.

So what transpired in Suhita's meeting...

Suhita set up her meeting stating her objective—to discuss delays in implementation. She called both leaders together and tabled her thoughts. She restated her cares and got them to state theirs. This was a great step as it got them to remember the central care of this project.

She went beyond her stories and assessments she held about each of these leaders. Instead of tabling some data and assertions, she tabled timelines and delays. She asked questions of relevance about impact of delay, explored options for each of their reservations and above all expressed how the delays impacted her.

Suhita found her agency to impact and figure out the best possible way to move forward rather than stay frustrated and resigned!

So the practices for our first finger are to become aware of our assessments in any given situation and examine them. We practice grounding our assessments so we stay in touch with our agency and the world of possibilities. We learn to listen to our stories and examine them.

Some business situations are unpredictable and volatile so leaders need to keep moving ahead through grounding assessments and devising small steps as a way of addressing their care.

We also gather assertions for any situation as assertions and factual data is an important aspect that supports our stance, opinion and direction.

Practice 1

- Write 10 sentences on yourself.
- Write 10 sentences about a colleague.
- Check how many are assessments and how many are assertions.
- What does this reveal to you? What came easily to you? How many are assessments and how many are assertions?

Practice 2

Think of a situation or of a colleague where you know you hold negative assessments about them. Apply the grounding assessments questions and observe what shifts in your perspective?

What is enabled in you due to this shift?

What next actions can you take with this colleague?

What are you learning about yourself?

Practice 3

Consider a tough issue at work. It could be a situation with a team member, a peer or a customer/client.

Allow yourself to write down without censoring your thoughts around why the issue is tough for you, your thoughts and feelings about it. Write a page or two.

Now read it and spot the assessments.

Apply the grounding questions.

Additionally ask yourself what experiences, strengths and resources you have to address this issue?

What are the assertions you have on this situation?

What could be the smallest step to begin?

Are you equipped or ready, or do you need more time, support, thinking to scaffold you?

Is there an individual with whom you can talk this through with before you take action?

Reference

1. Brothers Chalmers. *Language and the pursuit of happiness*. Naples, FL: New Possibilities Press 2005.

Chapter 10

REQUESTS

Chitra led a team for software design and delivery. She and her team were preparing for a key client visit. There was work to be reviewed, new plans and a road map to be created and presented. She was overloaded and so was the team. She needed extra support in doing some tasks which perhaps she may get from another team in the same business. However Chitra's mind had assessments, stories about asking the other team for support. Her business head did not have the greatest equation with the other team's manager. Over the day Chitra found herself whining and grumbling to her boss and a peer. She was overloaded, overwhelmed and in a poor mood.

By the next day she decided to speak to the business head of the other team to spare one strong resource person to support her. She explained her cares around the client visit and answered all his queries and to her surprise he was cooperative. He offered her a good senior lead who was very skilled, and she was relieved. It freed up her time and her mind to know she had a great resource to support her for all the collaterals she needed to get ready. She began to feel more confident about handling the client visit as she was better prepared and at ease. She became more ambitious in the next few days. Gone were the stories of overwhelm and negativity. She had more energy to guide the team effectively.

In 'language' she made an action we call a request. She listened to the other team manager's questions, answered him and negotiated what he was committing to her. If she hadn't made a clear request, her future would be different, her mood would be resentful. In this language action of 'requesting' a colleague and getting him to promise a resource emerged a new possibility that may not have existed before if Chitra had worked alone in preparation for this meeting.

A request is when we seek assistance from another person to satisfy a concern that we have. (1)

- A request can satisfy our requirements.
- It creates an opportunity to address our concerns and hence create a new future.
- It is made in the present moment and invites a future action in the other.

Making effective requests is a significant language action for leadership. It drives others to work in the same direction that we, as a team, want to head towards. If we want results, we need to make requests.

When I first came across this content on requests it seemed rather trivial.

A request? What's the big deal? Don't we make requests all the time?

Making an effective request is a skill. Leaders often fail to do this and then they wonder why they don't get effective action from their teams. It is a skill because a request needs to be made while paying attention to the many elements listed below.

Elements of a Request

Speaker of the request: This is the person who is making the request. As the requestor, do we know what we want? Are we being clear and specific about what we require? Are we also clear about what we might not know and still need to find out?

Listener of the request: This is the person or persons to whom we make our requests.

Do they get it? Are they clear what we need? Is the request made to a specific individual or is it thrown into the air in the hope that someone will act on it? We all have been in many meetings where it is not clear who is going to act on what at the end of the meeting. There is no clear listener of the request.

We've all been in meetings where someone says: 'Attention all, the customer is coming in two weeks and we require these five reports. I hope these reports get done'. This is not a request. This is a sentence. A request is when we will say: 'Will you do this? This X date is when we require it and these specifics are what it needs to have'.

There is specificity and what I call conditions of satisfaction for the kind of report needed. As a requester and a speaker of that request, I need it done by a particular time and in a particular way. This means there is a standard that I might define.

Conditions of Satisfaction: These are some basic standards that a requestor may have:

- What is to be done?
- When?
- For whom?
- By whom?
- Why?
- What is the standard to be met?

The importance of these standards is also significant. At times the speaker or the listener does not pay enough attention to the discussion, yet commitments are made. This lack of attention leads to breakdowns in the task and relationships. This is one of the most common missing elements of a request. A shared commitment cannot exist without this element being fully attended to.

Shared background of obviousness: There is a shared background or context to the request that a listener and requestor have. Often, this shared obviousness of things is absent between the speaker and listener. Sometimes leaders assume shared understanding, they assume that the listener holds an expansive picture. Perhaps, the same one that the leader has. This causes discrepancies in understanding as well as communicating the request.

Creating this shared background and not leaving this to assumptions is an important move the leader needs to make. 'For the sake of what are we doing this?' is the question the leader must articulate as many times as required.

Mood of the request: Requests can be made in the mood of demand, arrogance and force. Requests can also be made in the mood of openness and dialogue. The requester's mood is significant as it can open or close the listening of the other.[1] Mood is a distinction from ontological coaching.

[1] I heard this is the Coaching for Excellence programme by the Institute of Generative Leadership and this distinction is in many course papers written by Bob Dunham. I also refer to Rafael Echeverrias's paper on 'Mood and Emotions', a Newfield Network paper.

The mood of the listener is equally important. Is the listener receiving the request in a mood of resentment? Are they resigned and feeling stuck? Are they curious and willing?

A leader will pay attention to this as the commitment given by the listener will need to be assessed through this lens.

Reframing the Meaning of a Request

My request story

I happened to come across an interesting course on leadership coaching. It looked challenging, powerful and stimulating. I got introduced to Bob Dunham and set up a conversation via Skype. At the time, I was running a business organization offering training and coaching services alongside a wellness centre that provided psychotherapy and other emotional wellness services that the public could access. I spoke to him about my concerns and my need to learn. He in turn shared his aspirations for The Institute of Generative Leadership USA and himself as a teacher.

Something within me was ignited. I wanted to go and study with him. A three-year course, at least two visits a year to the United States for learning and additional course fees. It all seemed very daunting given where I as in life at that time. I had many assessments around being obligated to others, that others won't agree to my requests and that it looks very small minded to be making such demands for a bursary. I would not be able to pay the fee and how rude it was going to sound to state my needs and ask for a discount.

I was plagued with many questions as I had a young family with kids who still benefited a lot from my active presence. How would my family cope with my absence multiple times a year? How would I make payments for such a fee?

I was filled with self-doubt. How would I study in a cross-cultural environment? Will I be able to monetize and use my learning effectively after I return? How will I make all this possible?

Night after night, I went to bed with questions and my mind filled with assessments and I didn't know how to move ahead. I spent the day oscillating between self-doubt and enthusiasm about giving myself this opportunity. Despite all my hesitation, I decided to make a request. I requested for a fee assistance, explaining my context of professional practice and earnings in India. He graciously agreed. He said he would be happy to have me on the course. He extended every possible support and kindness I could imagine.

My journey of learning had a new lease of life. I now wonder what if I hadn't made that request. My life would have been devoid of this learning, the wonderful coach community I belong to. I would not have met my teacher and experienced the care and generosity that came into my life.

We experience their support, generosity and their unique strengths because we made a request. Reframing this language action in this way has removed the word 'obligation' that we normally associate with the word 'request'. When we see requests in this light as a way of connecting to our colleagues, community or even a neighbourhood, we no longer need to hesitate to make them.

A request allows another to participate in our life and in our cares.

As a coach and therapist, I get so many requests for a conversation. Yes, they are many a times a monetary exchange. Does that mean that there is no satisfaction and it is all about the commercial exchange?

There is tremendous satisfaction when I am invited into someone else's life through a request. I can use my gifts and participate in their journey. I can add value to them in a small or big way. As human beings, we are wired to enjoy and find fulfilling rich moments in a relationship.

Many coachees and participants claim that it took away the stigma or assessments they held around requests being a sign of weakness, an imposition or an obligation. Requests allow participation in a shared future that you and the other are looking towards together.

Requests: REDs and GREENs

I have taken inspiration from language viruses that Budd and Rothstein outline and focused on the gender lens. (2)

Given women's typical adaptations of discounting their thinking, and being pleasing, perfect and passive, let's now see how it plays out as REDS in making requests.

1. Not making requests

We don't make requests because it is difficult to listen to a 'no'.

Some of us have a very contentious relationship with 'no'. We believe that when we make a request, the other person has to agree. We don't accept that 'no' is a legitimate response too. It becomes difficult to accept that a request can be declined. As a result, we don't make a request because our observer fears refusal or rejection.

In my courses many participants speak of their inability to say no to others. This again comes from our adaptive pattern to please others and keep everyone comfortable. With the inability to say no, is the other side of the coin too where we are also offended by others saying no. As a result we decide to not ask rather than be disappointed.

As a continuation of this RED some of us believe 'Others will think I'm incompetent'.

We think it is a weakness to be making a request because we have thoughts like:

'I should be able to do this'; 'I should know this'; 'I shouldn't be needing to ask for this piece of information'.

I have heard several women in technology say: 'I needed to know this. It is part of my role. How silly it will look to be asking for this!' This comes from our adaptation to be perfect, know it all and be very good at what we do. By requesting information or technical support they see themselves as less. There is great pressure to be seen as a 'I know it all'.

GREENs:

I will make requests.
'Yes' and 'no' may come my way.
I will invite the other to participate in a meaningful way.
I cannot know everything, it is okay to ask and learn.

2. 'I won't state what I expect'

'I know what I think but I'm not going to say it'. This is where the adaptation of passivity shows up. Women are not encouraged to be active and direct with what they want. We do not act on communicating what we need. We are then in a big private conversation around resentment—resentment that others don't understand us, that others do not bother about our needs and that we are sidelined.

A leader's inner chatter about her team member was: 'You should be knowing it. You've been in my team for so many years and you still don't know this? Why do I need to tell him?'

We hold our expectations secretly and imagine that the other has X-ray vision and X-ray understanding to read our minds!

GREENs:

I say what I expect and why.
I make direct requests.

3. Unclear requests

'Customer is coming, will you just handle all the logistics?' With this statement a leader thought she had made a request in the meeting. There was no clarity, specificity and conditions of satisfaction.

It is really a big place of breakdown in relationships and in organizations when there is an unclear request. People don't understand what we need. They don't know why we are not satisfied.

When we provide details to the listener, we're not doing it because they're stupid or that they cannot think. But communicating details in a request is setting up mutual understanding and hence satisfaction. Setting up requests with clarity, specificity and conditions of satisfaction is a relationship skill because you're setting up for mutual satisfaction.

GREENs:

I make clear, specific requests.
I state all conditions of satisfaction.
I ensure that the other and I have a shared, clear understanding. (How they listen to my request is my problem)

4. Inappropriate mood of the request

Some of us make requests apologetically. Almost like we're sorry to be making these requests. How do we appear to the other person if we're so apologetic? What is the significance that it has for the other?

Some of us are pleading. It was really interesting when someone I was coaching told me: 'I have this colleague who makes these requests and she's grovelling. I feel manipulated. The person is pleading like this and how can you say no? I felt sorry and I said yes'.

It is important to realize that a listener can feel manipulated with a pleading request. These approaches to requests come from the need to be pleasing, nice and be accepted by the other.

I remember many participants in my workshops making connections to their personal history: 'I have rarely seen my mother ask—I don't think she asked much. Just quietly kept doing her work'.

Some of us make requests in a very commanding manner. It appears as if refusal is not an option. So people fulfil the request resentfully or out of compliance. It is a worthy reflection for a leader deciding if he wants people's participation or just compliance?

A participant in my course shared how making requests enabled her to work on projects that she really wanted. 'Through learning about requests, I gained the confidence to talk to the management, explain my concerns and back them up with relevant data that I had collected. I requested for projects that I believed I could do better and saw them through successfully. Now my work speaks for me'.

GREENs:

I will make requests in a positive mood.
Moods of curiosity, openness and dialogue are important for me.

Powerful Requests Can Mean Powerful Outcomes

Santhya Vikram CEO of Yellow Train School shares how a request created magic for them.

'As our school community slowly started finding its roots and flourishing we had many questions on our mind. From where do we find more children? From where do we find parents who will be inspired by our alternate ideas and want to belong to this community? How do we accommodate all these children? The big question was—how do we build an infrastructure to meet these needs? How do we find the finances for a Middle and High school building that is required?

We had used up all our resources, ideas, well-wishers, literally everything that we had, to build what is now called the Phase 1 of our school. We could not operationally sustain if we had to go through only bank borrowings. Then came the real question of how do we manage? What is the solution for raising funds?

I had a feeling that our parent community were a valuable people to ask and to be open about our search. Sai and I explored the execution of this idea. We worked through all the details. We decided that we were going to ask people for interest free loans and whatever they could offer. We worked out the modus to do these requests, the different elements that would need attention.

I wrote a very personal letter which carried my request. I met parents in small groups and kept the mood personal and intimate. I shared the real picture of the school and its struggles and requested them to financially support the school out of choice and freedom. There was going to be absolutely no judgement about givers or non-givers. Even during the meetings, I felt such warmth and love and many people even came to tell me that in this vulnerability of asking for support they found strength and striving and this is precisely what moved them into action for the school.

What followed after these meetings in the form of mails, letters, real action and commitment from people moved me and has changed something forever in the spirit of the Yellow Train school. Of course, it changed the spirit of the financial pursuit too. After one of my meetings, in less than 20 minutes, someone went home and brought back the first cheque saying he wanted it to be the first cheque. One father who was leaving school to move back to the United States offered us his loan and said it gives him a feeling that something of theirs is still with the school. Now I see that so many families that have moved to other cities and countries have still left their loans with us. Apart from all these anecdotes, in less than 3 months out of the 200 parents we asked, there came a contribution of 1.6 crores as loan to the school. All were out of freedom and choice. The whole process was about making a powerful request'.

Practice 1

- Reflect on the requests you make or don't make.
- Where are you comfortable making them and where do you not make them? For example, compensation, new role, customer-facing responsibility?
- Examine your emotions and inner thoughts around making such a request?
- If you continue not making requests, how could it impact you?
- Where are you willing to begin making more requests?

Practice 2

- Which REDs did you identify with? With whom do you tend to fall into these RED patterns?
- Which GREENs are you willing to start practicing and why?

Practice 3

Are you willing to be bold with your requests? We need boldness for a request that seems big and perhaps not so easy to achieve? A courageous request is a leadership moment.

Go ahead, make it!

References

1. Brothers Chalmers. *Language and the pursuit of happiness*. Naples, FL: New Possibilities Press, 2005.

2. Budd Matthew and Rothstein Larry. *You are what you say you are*. New York, NY: Three Rivers Press, 2000.

Chapter 11

OFFERS

Gia was in a resentful mood when we met. Her role at work was watered down and not in correspondence with her competence. She felt her skills were underutilized. The team she worked with had morphed as the focus of the business had changed over a period of three years. Given what the business was doing now, her role was marginalized. She complained saying she was confused about staying or leaving. She was in a mood of resentment.

I was struck by how articulate Gia was. She had a wide exposure to the entire software life cycle, had dabbled in pre-sales as well as software quality enhancement. Clearly, I was in the presence of a person with a range of skills and exposure to small and large software development projects.

I said to her: 'Gia I get that you are disenchanted with the situation at work. I wonder what you have offered your boss in terms of what else you can do?' She looked at me like I had asked her a bizarre question. True to her expression she remarked:

'What can I offer? They know me, they need to offer me something'.

I explained my question to her. 'I get that they have to offer you a role. They have offered you something and you are unhappy because you underutilized. Are there areas in the current business where you can add value? Are there areas where your unique strengths in the software life cycle can be leveraged in a way that would serve your team better? Do you have special value to add in addressing some pain area in your team? Can you offer yourself there?' She was gobsmacked with my questions!

Stimulated from our coaching conversation, she decided to try this approach. She knew she needed to do her homework first.

She thought through areas where she felt there were significant breakdowns in the team and across teams too. She identified two such areas where she could add value and save the team lots of time and wastage.

She set up a conversation with the business head and offered herself in both these areas—one as an active resource and another as a consultant to another team. Her business unit head was impressed with her thinking. He crafted a role involving her spending 50 per cent time on these other roles apart from the key role that she was anyway delivering on. When she began offering her services in this newly created role, she found high degree of visibility for her competence, received much more appreciation and once again became re-engaged in her work.

The next time I met her she seemed highly driven, motivated and involved. There was no talk of confusion or looking for a job change.

An offer is what we make to satisfy a need either in the other person, a team or an organization.

Just like a request, an offer has many elements. (1) There is a speaker, a listener and there are conditions of satisfaction that you are going to meet for the other when you make an offer. Offers need to be specific, just like requests.

Making an offer can change others' and our own future. It is a powerful language action.

If the other accepts our offer, we negotiate how to move forward and participate together in the future. The other has a choice to decline our offer too. In Gia's case, the business unit head accepted her offer as he saw value and relevance in what she had offered.

A valuable offer can change others' and our own future.

The value and relevance is significant in whatever offer we make. That is an important basis of acceptance or rejection of your offer.

Reframing Offers

1. Offers allow us to recognize and value our competence, experience and skills

Gia had some great skills and competence that could serve her team.

At times we have skills that can address a crisis or breakdown. At times we know people or a network that could solve the problem and we can make an offer to leverage our network. Making offers allows us to use what we have in ourselves for the sake of adding value.

2. Offers are a way of participating and being a contribution

Savitha offers her time in tending to the accounts of an old age home.

Rashmi offers to manage the kitchen twice a month at the school that her child attends.

Sandip offers to create the background score for a film an NGO is making.

These are wonderful examples of being a contribution or expanding yourself as you participate in something bigger than what you may do as an individual contributor.

3.   Offers are about caring for the other's cares

When Gia offered herself to do two different roles—she was taking care of herself, no doubt. However, she also aligned herself to the care of those two other teams and that is what struck a chord possibly. People take up our offers because what we offer them takes care of their own care—it is viewed as valuable. We are seen as individuals with an initiative.

4.   You are an offer

As a professional, we bring skills, competence and expertise. As an entrepreneur you may design and craft services or products that others find valuable. All of this, is in the realm of Doing.

As a human being with potential, values and unique strengths you are an offer.

Sonal is a therapist. She brings skills and competence to every session with her clients.

She provides a space for clients—that is caring, compassionate and non-judgemental. Her acceptance of who they are, attitude of listening and reflection comes from a deeper knowledge that she values, and respects her clients for who they are. It is not always that there is a solution for a client's issue. Yet, Sonal is an offer to her clients because of who she is.

I find it useful to think that you the person are also an offer. This is in the realm of the Being. We as human beings with our values, capacity to listen, understand, craft and design, and bring our personal qualities to a relationship or a problem are an offer. It's not always about what we do for another, but who we are and who we can be for another.

You the person are an offer. This is in the realm of being. With your unique set of values, your capacity to listen, understand, craft and design you bring your personal qualities to a relationship or to problem solving. It is not always about what we do for another— but who we are and who we can be for another.

Organizations lay great emphasis on tasks, deliverables and therefore on the doing. We forget that Doing is fuelled by the Being that we are.

Divyashree was heading a small OD team in an MNC. As a leader she was exceptional in how she organized herself and her team. As an OD head her interaction was with HR business partners as well as the business itself. She would hold many meetings, ideation conversations and project conversations both within her team and across mixed functions too. Some of these meetings would turn conflicted and became aggressive in their mood with colleagues who challenged each other. Some meetings had people pulling in different directions as each had an agenda as well as political undercurrents.

Divyashree had superior 'process skills'. Process skills are those that enable us to tap into and sense the internal process and energy of people in a room through our listening, presence, body language and also through our questions. She maintained a sense of pleasantness, calm and capacity for enquiry into another's thinking, slowly drawing them out to express their needs. Process skills are about who we are which influence what we are able to do. Most good facilitators have this skill. Divyashree made an impactful difference in every meeting she was part of because of who she was as an individual. Who she was enabled all that she did. She was the offer, not just what she did in her role!

Offer REDs and GREENs

1. Not making offers at all

This is about doing what we're asked to. The adaptation of passivity.

At times this comes from low self-esteem where we believe we do not have too much to offer. We are anxious if we will be able to deliver what we offer, hence we rather not offer. Some of us hold assessments that as a team member we are there to work on instruction and direction.

GREENs:

Look at places you can contribute and do it.
Look at strengths and gifts you have and spaces that can value them.
Show up—raise your hand and volunteer.

2. Not making relevant and valuable offers

There are some domains where we make lots of offers and some domains where we don't make offers at all.

Very often the places we avoid are precisely the domains that we need to be making offers in!

Offers bring us visibility. When Gia offered her expertise in two spaces, she had new visibility. We can say: 'I can present at that conference so that we can showcase what we have created'. If there is an event, we can say: 'I would love to speak on this topic'. This is when we are making visibility happen. We are opening a space for more possibilities because we meet, share, are seen and heard. We are experienced through our offers, and through offers we will add value.

GREENs:

Make offers that matter to your team and business.
Make offers to resolve the pain points of your team.
Make offers that bring you visibility.

Women and Offers

It is useful to reflect on where women make or do not make offers. It is connected to our adaptations of pleasing, passivity and stopping ourselves from showing up as smart.

I notice that women are making offers in places that 'fit' in our gender roles—where we nurture, show care and concern or are making use of our organizing skills.

We must make offers in the domain of our care and others' care. Your offers shape your professional identity and how you will be seen in your organization.

We are not making enough offers which fit in roles that connect with power, intellect, strength, finances or influence.

Selvi was a project manager in an MNC. She has shared earlier on calls with the group that her challenge was to be seen as a technical go-to person in her business.

She shared that she decided to make an offer to design momentos for a large team event, which had rewards and recognition as part of the event. I had a few questions for her which got her thinking about her offer. As a project manager, what care of her boss was she taking care of by this offer? Could anyone else in the team have taken care of this if they were given ideas? How was she shaping her public identity by this offer? Is that satisfying for her? If she had to shape herself as a technical go-to person, what offers would she need to make instead of this one?

I was once speaking to a diversity and inclusion leader in a leading German software organization and she lamented that she was fed up seeing women always offering to play assistant, do administrative activities on a team or be the first to organize games and food at team events. She said, 'When am I going to see these ladies say "I want to lead this client meeting"; "Pull me into that crisis call with the customer"; " Sales is fun let me try that out"?'

Practice 1

Given your role and your cares, answer these for yourself as a way of keeping yourself on track.

- What domains am I not making offers in—financial, technical, leading in a power role?
- How does this impact how I am viewed by peers and bosses?
- What are my hesitations about?
- What offers can I make that leverage my unique strengths?
- What offers get me visibility and are close to power centres?
- Can I make offers in the space of my care?

Sometimes our offers are too small as we try to play safe. Our inner critic plays loud.

Imagine a big offer you can make which you will deliver by working with others as a team. It is an offer that will shift how you are seen. You lead the entire offer but you will play with others for delivering it! Any ideas?

Have a conversation with an ambitious colleague who can support you in shaping this offer.

Go ahead, make your offer!

Reference

1. Brothers Chalmers. *Language and the pursuit of happiness.* Naples, FL: New Possibilities Press, 2005.

Chapter 12

PROMISES

When someone makes a request, there is a speaker of that request and there is a listener to whom that request is being made. The response to a request can be a promise which the other person makes to us. If it is the other who is making a request, then it is we who are making the promise.

When a promise is made, it means that the promisor has understood what they need to deliver and what the conditions of satisfaction for the other are. When they say 'yes' we believe they have full intention to fulfil it, are sincere about it and have the competence to deliver on the promise.

Promises and agreements underlie everything that we do with others. They are the most basic level, the 'actual action' that we use in very different ways as we do what we do in the world.—Chalmers Brothers (1)

When we promise, we are committing to produce a particular future action or result for ourselves or for another.

More than any other language action, the way we make and keep our promises or commitments has a profound impact on the outcomes in business as well as in relationships. This is because the way we manage our promises is connected to our public identity—the way we are seen by others.

Promises and How Others Listen to Them

A promise exists in the 'listening' that we have for one another—the listening of that which is explicit and implicit in the relationship with the other. (2)

My team member takes leave very often and does not inform me about it in advance. She often says one thing and does another. When she promises that she will come back after three days of leave, it does not land as a promise for me. This is because she has made promises earlier that she has not kept. In my listening of her, there is distrust of the commitments that she makes.

But sometimes even when a promise isn't actually made, it is listened to by the other. It is listened to on an implicit level. It is held implicit also in the relationship with the other.

My daughter says there is a fabulous theatre performance she wishes to go for on the weekend. I hear her out with attention and tell her: 'Sure, let's see on Saturday, okay?' My daughter goes off feeling very happy. Her listening is that 'Mamma said yes she will take me'. In her listening, she hears a promise, although I didn't make one.

Promises exist in the mind of the listener. They lie in the hidden unspoken agreements that are unstated in relationships. This is very tricky because when we do not keep even such promises that are held in the 'listening' of the other, it still impacts our relationship and trust.

Trust is established in relationships based on the promises we make and those that are listened to too. The rigour with which we will evaluate what our response needs to be and how we will engage with the request made, ensures a continued trust in the relationship. In a conversation at work, especially no one may explicitly tell you that 'I trust you' or 'I don't trust you', but the assessments are always happening. At work our team members may be implicitly listening to our promises of taking care of their careers and their interests. When promises are not met, it leads to resentment and distrust.

Promises and Our Identity

There are four aspects specifically that get impacted when promises are met or not met. (1)

- Trust
- Relationship
- Success
- Self-esteem

The leader who broke a promise

I was coaching a senior manager who led a team of eight project managers and their teams in a complex and large scale software project. One of the outcomes he wanted was to be an 'inspiring leader'—someone who commands respect and loyalty so that teams are inspired to work with him.

I enquired with this leader if he would be willing to ask his team for a feedback. I decided to ask the team members about the expectations they had from him and build them into the coaching goals for the leader. He received feedback from his team within a week of asking.

The core of the feedback was that he just wasn't available to them. He hadn't realized that this was how they assessed him. They claimed that he was too busy meeting collaborators, peers and higher-ups. His team experienced unavailability, lack of contact and adequate feedback, and direction. They experienced being driven rather than guided and inspired. This was despite the fact that the rest of the organization saw them as a successful team already.

The leader made a promise to his team: 'This year, I will be more available'. He committed to meeting them more often and being available in the ways that they asked for. There was specificity to what he committed.

Then, this leader fell into his old pattern. He could not keep his promise and even lost sight of it. It had a big impact on trust, relationships and the success of his team because he promised but did not fulfil it. Very interestingly, and unknown to him, it had an impact on his self-esteem. It got revealed in coaching.

When we make promises and don't fulfil them, there is a part of us inside that knows that it is not fulfilled and we don't feel too great about it. There is a smallness that is experienced internally that may well be camouflaged and covered up. The world may never see it but we feel it internally.

There are some of us who make a lot of promises and cannot meet them. It erodes our self-esteem and our relationships. It is a slow and gentle process—it feels like soil erosion that happens with each gust of wind or water. Right from the smallest promise of telling our family that we will be home by 6pm, but always coming in at 8pm or telling our team consistently about something and consistently not doing it. There is a smallness that we feel within ourselves.

Chalmers Brothers goes on to present the following three types of promises.

- **Strong promises**: These are promises that we are absolutely committed to. A strong promise is one that will be backed up with our energy, efforts and plans. We make concerted actions to fulfil it. Many of us make strong promises in certain domains of our life. I made a strong promise around women and leadership. I said that I would create an online course for women. It was a strong promise I made to myself and the world, worked at it and made it happen.

- **Shallow promises**: These look like strong promises but there is a caveat that we don't always reveal or perhaps are unaware of. The caveat could be our mood, difficult circumstances that stretch us and personal convenience. For example, a shallow promise that I made is around eating sweets. I don't want to eat them. But sometimes I might be tempted and eat them. Then I say: 'No really it's okay. Next week I needn't eat'. It's a shallow promise.

- **Criminal promises**: These are promises we make which we have no intention to fulfil and are aware of it while making the promise. Some years ago I made a lot of criminal promises in the area of health. I never attended to it. In my head I'm saying 'Health is very important. I will do this, I will do that', but there is a part of me inside that knows I'm not going to follow through on it. I had to face it and ask some tough questions to myself. I stopped myself from making criminal promises.

In my courses, over 90 per cent of the women report making criminal promises to themselves—a pattern that is hard to ignore. They report that these are mainly in the domain of health, personal development and finances. It stems from the core assessment that a lot of women hold:

'I am not important'. This often translates as 'My needs are not important. Other's needs come first'. Anyone with low self-esteem will know the number of promises made to themselves that they have broken.

Ria was a HR professional with over 12 years of work behind her. She lived with her in-laws and had two kids, six and three years old. She shared that every week she would tell herself that she would go for a walk in the morning and never ended up doing it. There always seemed to be something that filled up her space—either in-laws needs or her children's lunch boxes or getting them ready before going to work. She lamented how grossly overweight she was and how she didn't feel good looking at herself in the mirror.

Boli grew up in a traditional family with a small-town upbringing. She was a manager with a KPO and led quite a large team. With over 16 years of experience, she earned well too.

But she knew nothing of her personal finances. Having seen that it is a weak area for her, she had recently attended a course on personal finance awareness held in her company. Yet, she procrastinated on getting a hold of her own finances. Everything was left to her father who made all decisions in this area. Every month when her salary was credited, she would tell her self: 'This month I surely will look into it'.

Many of us make shallow promises, perhaps towards extended family, spouses, friends and sometimes to children.

Of course, by realizing this aspect, one can make amends and repairs. This is a key to rebuild trust in the relationship.

Criminal promises remain criminal as long as we deny and push them under the carpet. Acknowledging our criminal promises is the start. Revisiting our cares can also help. Clarifying and renewal of our commitments to our cares often help us make strong promises.

Similarly, shallow promises often come from mindless commitments to others, lack of time to process why we are making promises and lack of attention to the relationship where we are making them. Being mindful of these aspects supports the shift to strong promises or no promises where you don't want to make one.

Managing Promises Is a Relationship Skill

There are times in life when we cannot fulfil our promise. It is not about keeping every promise. It's about taking full responsibility for managing our promise. It is useful for us to remember that promises are not written in stone. We can go back and alter them in a responsible manner.

When we hold a promise, we take full responsibility for the fact that we've made that commitment. The action of taking responsibility means we renegotiate, go back and keep people informed. The moment we know that we are unable to meet our commitment we tell them. I learn to actively manage my promise and in doing that I manage my relationship with the other. I show you that they matter to me and I care about our relationship.

Promises Not Kept Are Not the Same as Expectation Not Met

We sometimes confuse promises with our expectations from others.

Human beings are expectation machines! We expect from partners, families and team members, and we treat those expectations as promises! Then we become resentful because people are not meeting them. Often, the difficult question that I have to ask in coaching conversations is to ask the coachees: 'Did they promise you this?' Their response is: 'No, but that's what's supposed to be done'. Sometimes we have reached the highest level of resentment in that relationship without ever having any exchange of promises. There hasn't been any conversation on promises.

It is wise for us to begin making this separation both in our personal and professional lives. There are expectations, there are promises and there is a conversation that connects these two spaces. It is useful to become aware that many times we don't hold these conversations but we hold people responsible for what they should do, must do and haven't done.

When we begin to understand that there are three pieces to this aspect—expectations, promises and conversations, it is a great start to managing relationship breakdowns and repairing them. As leaders, we can take responsibility to analyse and see if some aspect of these three was left unattended. We can attend to the piece we need to, rather than hold an attitude of blame and judgement.

Promises REDs and GREENs

Using a gender lens I am building the typical REDS women fall into. (3)

1. RED: Making promises when you are unclear about what is expected as the outcome

If we're in an organizational life, we're constantly receiving requests—verbally, via mails, via customers and all kinds of ways. People are expecting promises to be made. At times we are saying 'yes', when we don't even know what is needed. Sometimes in coaching when this is revealed, people ask me: 'Won't I look stupid if I'm clarifying and asking so many questions before I say yes?' I'm wondering 'Won't you look stupid when it is not achieved or when you have not delivered what the person is asking for?' Very often we feel compelled to say yes when someone is asking us something. We think that it is a speed test. Some of us have those assessments so a delayed response is not an option we give ourselves.

Veronica was a tech lead reporting to a project manager. She identified that she always said yes from her need to please. She assumed that her manager will be offended if she declined any request and that she would be seen as 'not good enough' because she could not fully understand what he needed. It was her assumption that her manager always knew with clarity what was needed. He didn't.

She would do a piece of work and realize that it would not fulfil what he asked for. She realized that unclear requests are incomplete or ineffective conversations and need to be completed. She began asking more questions, paraphrasing her manager, ending the meeting with summarizing her understanding and telling her manager that she will do a small piece of work and check if she is in the right direction. This was a great idea as it saved her a great deal of time and effort.

This is the first RED—promising when we are unclear, not knowing how to pause and not knowing that we have other possibilities than a yes. 'No' is a legitimate response and so is 'I will revert after some thought'. We can also make a counter offer of what we can manage to achieve. We can also do what Veronica did—work in small parts to see if we are in the right direction.

GREENs:

Learning to ask questions is significant.
Clarifying and asking the requester what would satisfy them.
Query the other on timelines, quality, expenses, authority and role.
Understand the context of the request—for the sake of what is this being asked of you.
Take your time to respond. Pausing is important.

2. RED: Not declining

It's important to decline promises in some areas, but we don't. Conditions of satisfaction of the other may be clear and the request may be specific. It may still call for a decline for other reasons—time, other commitments made earlier, role conflict etc.

In September 2018 I ran an online event on the topic 'Increasing capacity and managing overwhelm'. I had leaders from amongst us and some coaches from abroad do short sessions on this topic. The most common issue women identified with in realm of over-whelm was their lack of capacity to say 'no'. It emerged that saying no was seen as rude, not pleasant enough and for some women next to impossible.

In my workshops I do a paired somatic experience of saying no to a request and the partner gives you feedback of how the other showed up. Some women speak so softly they can barely be heard. Some others have a collapsed and scared body as they say no. Some have shifty eye contact.

There is so much socio-cultural messaging for women especially around not declining. This comes from our adaptation of pleasing and adapting to others. 'It doesn't look nice'; 'How will I appear?'; 'What kind of identity am I building?'; 'Am I this person who is always saying no?'

Not declining has an impact on our time, priorities and energy. We and our time are finite and it is important we remember that.

Are we allowing ourselves to choose? Are we asking: 'how does this connect with my care?'; 'How does this connect with my schedule and capacity?' Practicing a GREEN in this area is the only way of building this muscle.

GREEN:

Declining is a legitimate response and is often needed.
Being over committed is not for me.
I choose comfort over overwhelm.
I am committed to managing my capacity.

3. RED: Broken promises and no commitment to care

Making criminal promises and shallow promises which are not connected with our personal care impacts our self-esteem.

Over 90 per cent women in my courses have come back saying they make criminal promises around their health. I get that as I have been there myself for many years with putting absolutely no thought to it. Women give examples of eating poorly, not exercising ever, not doing health checks and staying with symptoms for a long duration without going to the doctor. Many identify that they had women in their family who did exactly that.

Savi was one such leader. The promises module was a turning point for her. She put health as her first care when we did the care exercise and reflection. Over the 1-year programme, the group saw her making big changes in her daily routine, eating habits and making time for exercise. Savi began walking to work in the morning, persuaded her spouse into walking each evening with her. She hired extra help at home to make space for these new actions. She says she shopped for groceries differently and hired a cook for the mornings so she could carry two to three small packed meals from home. At the closing of our one-year group, she had lost 15 kg of weight and was exploring running a half marathon! Connection with our care and making strong promises really powers up our actions!

GREENs:

I make strong promises in the area of my care.
I am finite and so I take care of myself and my time.
I say no to others so I make time for my promises and cares.
I grow my self-esteem by doing what I say I will do.

4.   RED: Promises broken by others

Unfulfilled promises lead to breakdown of trust. It causes resentment.

In teams when broken promises becomes the group culture, team members are frustrated. There is low trust and care for each other. It is the start of personal games with people becoming resentful and pulling each other down.

A powerful move to make when promises are broken is to make a responsible and dignified complaint. (1) This is a respectful conversation where we discuss commitments made and the consequences of promises not kept. The focus is to take care of the broken promises in a way that the task goals are met and the relationship is protected too. We need to pay attention to context, our emotions and moods here. Learning to make such a conversation is vital as it encourages trust, accountability and personal responsibility in teams.

Women many a times do not do this action as they are pleasing others and are concerned about hurting the other. Once again our adaptation of pleasing as well as being passive can get in our way.

I believe learning to assert ourselves in a respectful and dignified way allows good use of our voice.

GREENs

I will enquire rather than judge others when promises are broken.
I will hold a mood of respect and still raise a complaint.
I keep my dignity and the dignity of others in a conversation.
I focus on asking questions rather than becoming resentful.
I choose relationship over distrust therefore I will clarify.

5. Red: Not clarifying the promises we receive from others

Let's assume we wish to create a team that has a culture of responsible promises. When others make a promise and use language such as 'I will try', 'maybe', 'possibly' or 'perhaps' or are silent and unresponsive, as a listener to such promises, we have a responsibility to clarify these responses rather than be passive about it. If we don't, we are sure to end up feeling resentful when the person does not finally deliver.

When we fall back into our adaptation of pleasing others or being passive and going along, we do not ask questions based on the others' weak responses. We are invested in looking good and not wanting to be judged.

To build a culture of commitment, we have four valid responses from the other that we can accept. (1)

These four are as follows.

1. **Yes**: This means acceptance or yes I will do it.

2. **No**: Decline. It is clear that they are not making a promise. We know that 'no' is a legitimate response too.

3. **Commit to commit**: They say that they will revert to you within a specific time and they do that. Sometimes people need to assess

that they can make a commitment and we should provide them that option. 'I will revert to you at...' is a practice.

4. **Counter offer:** They decline our first request, but they make another offer to us of what they can manage to commit. We check to see if this suits the conditions that satisfy us.

These four responses do not allow any fuzziness or unclearness and aim at being clear and specific. We wish to stay away from any assumptions and want to provide everyone with a chance to fulfil commitments made to us.

GREENs:

I look for a clear yes or no; if unclear, I ask again.

I am aware of body language along with verbal communication.

Yes, no, commit to commit and counter offers are responses I use and encourage others to do the same.

I clarify responses so I and the other can remain in a trusting relationship.

I remain open and explore the options with others.

Promises are about designing our life

Bigger Promises
Bigger Impact
Expansion

The promises we make as well as the manner we execute them change the way we are perceived in the world. They shape our public identity.

This is also true in connection with promises we make to ourselves.

A bigger promise for myself

It was May of 2016, I was in a beautiful wooded area of the Colorado Mountains. I was excited because I could feel in my bones a stirring I could not comprehend yet. I was there for a conference. Being a psychologist and having studied so much about developmental stages in life, I knew that this was one such stage. It wasn't a clear thought—just felt a sense and understanding within me. I was restless.

I was spending a few days in the nature place and decided that I needed to bring clarity for myself. What better way than a conversation? My dear colleague and friend Kobe Bogaert was there. I still remember, vividly, the basement space we met in. It was 8am, much before everyone came in for breakfast. I was excited and had come to meet him with a sheet of paper on which I had scribbled away thoughts coherent and incoherent.

I shared my thoughts, he asked me questions. We spent over an hour.

It emerged that I wanted to be a force in the women leadership landscape in India. I wanted to build a community. I wished to create a platform to share, discuss and learn together. I wanted more women to access my work. I wanted to do long-term work with organizations in this space. I wanted to curate ideas, and grow myself and others.

Such a profusion of thoughts and ideas burst forth. Kobe held space for me in the way he does best—with a spirit of encouragement and abundance. He pointed me to some fine examples of women leaders who may have done similar work. He asked great questions as any good coach would.

It was clear to me that I was ready to hold a new promise. A bigger promise—one that would expand the scope of what I offer in the world, shape my identity differently, and stretch me as a learner, an entrepreneur and an expert in my field.

I made a promise in the women in leadership space that would be shaped with who I now was—a psychotherapist, an organizational consultant, a generative leadership coach, a transactional analyst and a woman leader wanting to create impact in my country. A bigger promise was born over a few more conversations with myself, my coach and colleagues.

This was a moment of design. From this bigger promise was born Step Up the programme, Lead Powerful Live Mindful—an online group for Professional Women in India, and now this book. I articulated my promise to several people who are committed to my learning and growth. I think that was a significant step to having other witnesses to my bigger promise and a new design mood I held for myself. Each time I slipped or felt stuck, these awesome people reminded me to move into a mood of curiosity, learning and ambition.

For any professional, the *bigger promise* conversation is worth visiting each year along with one's cares. It allows us to review our achievements in connection to what we care about and realign with new promises where we can commit our time, energy, resources and learning in the year to come. There are times when I have told myself that each year may not be a year for an even bigger promise. There are some periods we wish to slow down for renewal, consolidation or just for learning and it is wise for us to make these choices.

While expanding towards a bigger promise, the SELPH needs examining. Typically all our disempowering narratives and assessments get triggered as we are invited outside of our comfort zone or normal flow in life.

In the courses that I lead, articulating a bigger promise is an experience that is quite daunting especially for emerging women leaders. Having used this process with many women I am aware it can cause a stir. One of my clients said it was: 'Like having a storm in a teacup'. A bigger promise can bring up our inner critic voice that tells us we are not good enough. Tara Mohr in her book

Playing Big speaks about this as a typical response to transition and changing one's identity.

While for some it brings on doubt and anxiety, others are able to approach this conversation with curiosity and ambition.

This is my guidance to design and support yourself through the bigger promise experience:

- Centre yourself each time you begin this exploration so you can bring in a mood of curiosity and ambition. This does not mean an absence of anxiety. Allow the other two moods to prevail.

- Create your bigger promise not just in your mind or on paper, but importantly through conversation. Designing this piece needs conversations with mentors, sponsors and a supportive peer perhaps. Seek them out.

- Make an inventory of your strengths and learning edges as you plan because it will help you ground how you need to manage the bigger promise.

- Create small steps in the plan towards your bigger promise and define a timeline that does not make you anxious.

- See the journey being as important as the final destination. It helps us see ourselves as dignified learners at all times.

- Bigger promises can be daunting and we can lose energy. Set up an accountability partner who walks with you. Set up a structure of how you will use their support. I normally suggest a weekly or twice a month connect depending on the kind of promise you need to execute.

- Practice all your GREEN mantras—they are vital.

- Get yourself a coach if required.

When we begin to shape our promises in alignment with what we care about we begin to shape our identity in the world.

I invite you to do a reflection on the promises you make through the practices listed here.

Practice 1

Reflect in what domains you are making strong, criminal and shallow promises in your life.

Domain	Type of Promise you are making. Strong/shallow/criminal/No promises
Spouse/partner	
Children	
Extended family	
Financial health	
Friendships	
Health	
Fun and relaxation	
Spiritual learning	
Pursuing a hobby	
Personal development	
Professional development	
Self-respect and dignity	
Social responsibility/community work	

These questions may support you:

- What does this reflection reveal about your promises and care?
- How come you are making these shallow and criminal promises in these domains?

- Who are you trying to satisfy by making these promises? (Sometimes we are satisfying the inner parental voice in us which says we should make these promises)
- What has got impacted due to criminal and shallow promises—trust, self-esteem or relationships?
- What do you need to change in order to make shallow promises strong or not make them at all?
- What would happen if you stop making those criminal promises?
- What would you need to change to convert your criminal promises to strong ones?

Practice 2

When a request is made, I stay aware that I have options to respond.

I pause and breathe; I take my time.

I practice any of these four to build my muscle for varied responses

Yes, no, commit to commit and counter offer.

Practice 3

Your bigger promise.

Are you ready to hold something much bigger in terms of a professional commitment for yourself?

These reflections may support your exploration:

- What is my current role? What is the impact of this role in my business/organization?

- What 'care' of mine is the current role serving?

- If it isn't fully serving a professional care, what would?

- What is that unique offer I have to make that adds value and uses my competence?

- In what domain/space do I feel ready to expand my role? What could an expanded role look like?

- How will this expansion serve me?

- What are my strengths and learning edges that I need to keep in mind for my bigger promise?

- Who do I need to enrol in this conversation so I move ahead towards a bigger promise?

- Who do I have in my network of support who can support me in arriving at my bigger promise?

- Am I willing to be in a mood of curiosity and design so this new and bigger promise emerges?

References

1. Brothers Chalmers. *Language and the pursuit of Happiness*. Naples, FL: New Possibilities Press, 2005.

2. Dua Sameer. *Declaring breakdowns powerfully creating a future that matters, through 6 simple steps*. New Delhi: SAGE Publications, 2016.

3. Mathew Budd and Larry Rothstein. *You are what you say you are*. New York: Three Rivers Press, 2000.

Chapter 13

DECLARATIONS

A declaration is something that is said by someone with authority and when they say it, it brings something into being that wasn't there before. (1)

In a cricket match when the umpire says 'out', it's a declaration. When he says 'out' a new reality exists that the person is out of the game. It is true even when a judge in the court of law declares a verdict. What wasn't there before suddenly comes into existence because that person has the authority to say so. In an organization, when a CEO or a manager says: 'You are out of your job. You're being fired', it is a declaration.

Before I held a promise on my work in women in leadership, my declaration was that: 'I am going to play in this space of women and leadership, and I will be a powerhouse coach for women in the mid to senior management level'.

Before I made this declaration, this clear direction didn't exist because I am the authority in this matter of choosing a direction and a focus for myself.

Declarations are the most generative of all the language actions as they create something new. With a declaration, a whole new set of actions and possibilities comes forth. Using declarations, we establish personal leadership as well as leadership in organizational life. (2)

When we make declarations, there are four primary actions. (2)

We either **open or initiate something**. When a leader makes a declaration about what the organization will achieve as goals in the year, it opens a new possibility. The leader initiates a set of actions in connection to making this happen.

We make declarations that **may close or conclude something**. I once worked with this person in their business, where they made declarations about me not being worthy of the role and an association with them. I believe they held some bias and some ungrounded assessments about me. After much reflection and conversations the declaration that I needed to make was: 'I conclude my relationship with this person and organization because I am not granting authority to them to make this declaration'.

We make declarations to **resolve something**. This declaration is about being clear of a direction. For example, organizations that approach me and say: 'I want this long list of results to be achieved in this really short time frame. You can push them as much as you like, do whatever you need to do, but we want this change to happen quick'. My declaration is that I cannot work with organizations that don't think of sustainability at the core. Transformational shifts in leadership take time. I have no formula or magic to use.

We may make a declaration just **to evaluate and assess**. This is about orienting us a certain way, either toward or away from certain possibilities. I remember when my care became clear,

I decided to step down from the board of a training and certifying organization I was part of. I declared that it no longer aligned with what I wanted to do. It oriented me away from a possibility I was otherwise involved with.

Some significant declarations Chalmers Brothers suggest for leaders are as follows.

Yes: A declaration to commit.
No: A declaration not to commit.
I don't know: A declaration to be a beginner, a learner.
I apologize: A declaration to take responsibility and offer a recourse.
Thank you: A declaration to be in a mood of gratitude.
I am: A declaration of who we are.

Two declarations I see of great of significance for women are as follows.

1. I am: A declaration of identity

This is often a very significant aspect of my work with women leaders. The need to relook at the definition of themselves, their identity. 'I am' is a primary or core declaration that is at the heart of our being.

I was recently on a coaching call with four women leaders. The topic we were discussing was the inner critic. This leader criticized herself for not grasping quick enough, not doing something fast enough and not doing things to the standard or quality she expected of herself. At the core of her identity was the declaration: 'I am not good enough'. This is the primary declaration that was not serving her. On the coaching call we had to unravel the assessments she held on to and for her to make a new declaration of 'I am enough and I am learning'.

Many of the GREEN mantras we have identified before are powerful declarations. There are many personal declarations that are useful:

I am a strong and ethical leader.
I am a good learner and I am learning all the time.
I am a balance of power and compassion in my leading style.
I am an authentic person.
I am good enough.

Think about how it feels to say these statements out loud. What sort of context for functioning are we creating for ourselves? These are ways of creating a new way of being.

When leaders make these declarations and hold them with conviction I notice they begin to shape their public identity differently. They seem to move with confidence and potency in their actions. They stand tall. Especially senior leaders begin to appreciate and integrate both the masculine aspects of power, action and certainty with feminine styles of compassion, authenticity and creativity.

We all have the power to declare and bring about the grandest version of the greatest vision we ever had about ourselves

- Neale Donald Walsch

2. 'This is not working'

A declaration that is important for being in a mood of design and being able to call out something to be improved.

This declaration, originally developed by Fernando Flores, is very significant for us women. Our adaptation of passivity, doing nothing as well as waiting for the right time, takes away power from us. Not being able to and willing to make this declaration causes delays in outcomes, breakdowns in relationships and toleration of mediocrity. In coaching I often have to point this out much more to women leaders than I need to do it with male leaders.

Something's wrong here.
This is no longer satisfactory.
This isn't acceptable.
This represents a risk.
This needs immediate attention.

Calling out a breakdown

Pooja was a project manager leading a delivery team of 180 people. She and her team were working on requirements for developing software for a client in the United States. She found that the client was working with certain uncertainties in their plans, and kept changing the requirement specifications. Each time they changed requirements, it meant scrapping some old work and redesigning and reworking some pieces. She had been struggling with rework coupled with tight deadlines and her team was exhausted as this had been the situation for over four months. She noticed that team members were falling ill due to undue stretch, many had low energy and motivation and some leads had not taken a break for months as they were burning at both ends—their teams as well as the customer. She had an option of asking for more resources but she realized that wasn't the issue. She needed to call out the 'breakdown' to the client.

'This is not working—this needs immediate attention' is the declaration she used. Over the next week, she decided she would travel with one of her project leads to the Unites States as she decided that they needed to understand why the requirements kept changing. What could the India team do to support the client in freezing requirements and a steady plan? She had to communicate that they cannot work with the constant changes and stretched deadlines. She needed to set boundaries and processes of how they could work, how monitoring would happen and the process for resolving conflicts. A big shift came about in how this project team continued to work. Thanks to the declaration made by their leader.

Many emerging women leaders lean towards care, nurture and tolerance. Learning to make this declaration as a leader serves us and our teams well. It invites us into a mood of ambition and excellence as we begin to see that outcomes and results are important because we as leaders are responsible for them. Whether it is calling out poor performance, stepping out of relationships that don't serve our outcomes, having tough conversations or standing up for ethical aspects of business are all valuable declarations that restore our power.

My friend and colleague Sameer Dua speaks compellingly on this in his book *Declaring Breakdowns* and provided steps to make changes once a leader has made this move.

Making Declarations Publicly

When we make declarations to others, not just privately, it takes challenge to a level higher because we are putting ourselves on the line. We show up as people who want to take responsibility and who will take responsibility in this area. Our output and outcomes are going to be assessed by another because we are making the declaration publicly.

Leaders and CEOs make public declarations all the time. However, it is important to realize that we can sometimes make baseless declarations that don't matter. We see this so much in the world of politics!

As we shape our identity as powerful leaders, we need to become more adept at making declarations publicly and hold ourselves accountable to deliver those.

When teams hear powerful declarations they are energized, see clarity and direction, and forces can then be rallied to achieve the promises held by the leader and the team.

Declaration REDs and GREENs

1. RED: Not making powerful declarations

We hesitate to say who we are often because we don't know. We have not clarified this question for ourselves. Since the self of the leader is where we lead from, not making a powerful declaration stops us from manifesting and showing up as a powerful leader.

A couple of years ago, I decided to take my final credentialing exams as a teaching and supervising transactional analyst in psychotherapy (TSTA). I declared it to a core group of colleagues and that one act got me moving. The exam was in Berlin the following year. It was a grilling and rigorous experience as one appears face to face with three different boards, each board consisting of professionals from my chosen field of Psychotherapy. It is an exam of identity formation and a place where I needed to declare who I am as a teacher and supervisor in psychotherapy, and why I do what I do. I needed to declare my philosophy of training and supervision along with my views on professional standards and ethical practice.

I arrived at much of this through a process of many, many months of reflection, conversations and tough questions that I had to struggle with over months. It was a powerful way to show up with an identity that was clearly articulated while being able to substantiate my actions as well as the philosophical underpinnings. My coach Gail expressed it well when she said it is a great practice in meeting eye to eye and declaring who you are.

After eight years of holding a provisional credential, it was a momentous occasion at the end of the journey to be declared a TSTA! A journey that strengthened me as I made so many declarations privately and publicly too!

Many women leaders find it hard to confidently make this move. It is connected to our adaptation of being passive, not giving ourselves the power to be significant and second guessing ourselves. Many emerging leaders hesitate to declare their values and beliefs and who they are as they think it is pompous to be speaking of who they are. The adaptation of needing to be perfect and learning it all before saying something tells them that they need to delay 'showing up'.

Many leaders who are yet to get comfortable being seen and heard do not make declarations publicly to their teams.

GREENs:

I will say who I am as a leader.
I will make declarations publicly so I have a witness.
I will take the support of a peer or mentor to support my journey.

2. RED: Allowing others to declare who we are

As women we give away authority to others to make choices for us and even to declare who we are. At times it is our parents, extended family, society and even our partners. I recollect this scene in the movie *English Vinglish,* where the husband in a public forum says: 'I think my wife was born to make laddus'. Or the movie *Queen* has several examples of family and social norms declaring how the character Rani would be in the world.

We allow others' choice and power in our declaration rather than making our own declarations. The question is how many times in our lives have we granted the authority to somebody else to make declarations for us?

GREENs:

I declare who I am.
I practice the 'I am' statements each day.
I will visit my personal and professional cares at least once a year and reaffirm my declarations.

3. RED: Declarations that have no feet, no ground

Some of us make declarations that have no feet. What I mean by that is that I may make big promises and declarations, but there is no backing up of any plan or any intention to actually do it. We act in ways that are inconsistent with our declarations. (1)

A person I know decided start a restaurant business. She declared that she would run a successful restaurant. She invested in the business in a big way without having the grounding in the know-how of the food business, running a kitchen or knowing to manage labour. The lady had a business partner who seemed to hold control, and because he had a better hold on the technicalities of the business the lady took a back seat in many aspects of the business.

The business incurred a huge loss. Declarations made need to be backed by clear business plans and direction. There is no space for whimsical actions and impulsivity. Assessments need to be grounded and breakdowns need to be called out upfront.

Powerful leaders put intention and direction into a declaration. A declaration is not just something that we wish or want to do. There is no magic in how we deliver on declarations. There is no place for light-hearted declarations in leadership. Declarations need a team, a plan, monitoring and accountability processes.

GREENs:

Declarations being specific is important.
Conditions of satisfaction—your own or others need to be specified.
Create a plan, monitor it and involve others if needed so you ground your declaration.
Keep checking out your assessments so you keep opening possibilities.
Let your declaration stand on firm ground.

Practice 1

This is a useful somatic practice I have facilitated with many women leaders. I call it 'I am here'. Given women's tendencies to be insignificant, discount themselves and carry a low confidence posture, this somatic practice builds strength in our voice and spine.

Stand in front of a mirror, your feet about 1 foot apart.

Spread your hand out to your side, palms facing upward, as if you are holding a large ball.

Look straight ahead at yourself in the mirror.

Say aloud: 'I am here' 3–5 times.

Repeat till you feel the energy in your body.

Do this is at the start of each day.

Practice 2

As leaders we get to declare few significant aspects at an individual level such as:

- What public identity we will shape for ourselves?
- What is important to us? We name our cares.
- Who we are as a leader—what are our personal standards?
- What is the kind of life we will lead?
- What is acceptable or unacceptable for us at an individual and professional level?
- Is there an area of life or a relationship where we wish to declare a breakdown? What next?

Journal on each of the aspects above.

In the mood of curiosity and resolve, I invite you to have a conversation with a peer or coach so you clarify these questions and arrive at few declarations of who you are and what you will do.

Participants of my workshop often report that this exercise allows them to feel taller and stronger, and they have a new voice as they speak to their teams, bosses and clients. Many say declaring 'this isn't working' was a starting point of rich conversations with a spouse, a boss or a client!

Practice 3

Declare a significant Step Up action every year for yourself. This idea is inspired from Tara Mohr's book Playing Big.

What is a Step Up action?

A Step Up action is a challenge action that will propel you to show up powerfully and differently that year. It needs to meet a certain criteria, which is as follows:

- You need to deliver on it in few months.

- You need to declare it publicly to those connected with it—your team, boss, family or your professional network.

- It needs to be something you will share in one short sentence: 'I will apply and set up three interviews for myself' or it could be 'I will lead a two-hour technical workshop for my team'; 'I will organize a meeting with the boss and the management team to broach a new topic that is of value for the team' or it could be that 'I will speak at a public forum or platform'.

- It needs to bring up your various REDs, which means it is a stretch and a challenge for you. If you're thinking of something that is not bringing up your REDs and some self-doubt, it is probable not a good Step Up action and you need to think of another one.

- It needs to put you in front of the people who need to see you, hear you and meet you. So that means significant stakeholders connected to your growth or people who need to notice you shaping your identity through this action.

- Above all, it needs to be aligned with one of your cares. Something that really matters to you.

References

1. Budd Mathew and Rothstein Larry. *You are what you say you are*. New York, NY: Three Rivers Press, 2000.

2. Brothers Chalmers. *Language and the pursuit of happiness*. Naples, FL: New Possibilities Press, 2005.

WIND BENEATH YOUR WINGS

I end this book with a significant chapter that has ideas to power up your Step Up journey! The two ideas here will build wind beneath your wings: *Developing men as allies and self-care.*

Developing Men as Allies

The men in our lives be they a spouse, partner, mentor, friend or a boss can be the juice that brings sweetness into our lives! They can bring stimulation, care, support, energy for action and fuel for our dreams.

Men as allies need to be grown, developed and nurtured. Male allies are what I call awakened men. My spouse is the wind beneath my wings and a big advocate of my work. It has taken some years of conversations and navigation to arrive here and it is a great place to step up from as I always know I can lean back for support! I have other men friends and colleagues who are allies and have great conviction in what I bring professionally to the table.

Given the socio-cultural context we live in, such awakened men are a small tribe, but growing fast. Jennifer Brown developed her *allyship continuum* (1) which I find very useful in allowing us to see what conversations and actions are needed in our life and work.

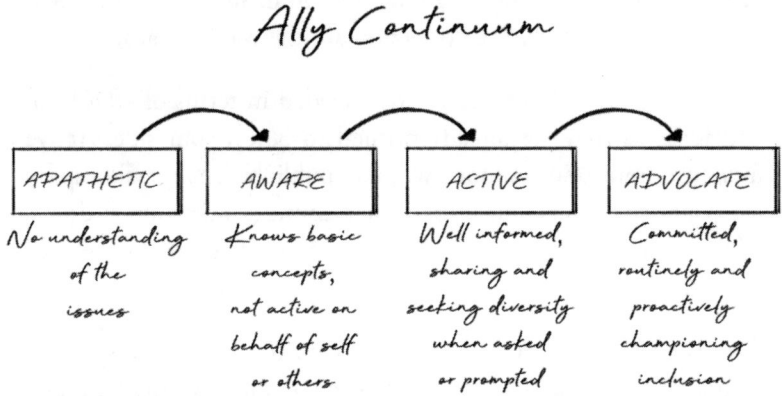

Ally Continuum

APATHETIC	AWARE	ACTIVE	ADVOCATE
No understanding of the issues	Knows basic concepts, not active on behalf of self or others	Well informed, sharing and seeking diversity when asked or prompted	Committed, routinely and proactively championing inclusion

Apathetic is the space of 'unawakened', in denial and not concerned with the gender view at all. Diversity and inclusion conversations at work help in this context as they shine the light on the existing unconscious biases. Women have learnt to bring up these conversations at home, which is an important place to begin. I have found that when I have led such conversations within organizations, they have been received very well as such conversations need to have a spirit of open experience sharing and respect. These conversations at work or home need to be devoid of blame, shame, judgement and self-righteousness. It is a delicate conversation to be handled with care. The onus is on women to invite men to these conversations.

With aware men, be at it at work or at home, we need to make clear requests so they can take action. We need to also offer supportive ideas so they learn to activate this aspect of their thinking which they may not yet be adept at. We become what we practice so allowing and providing for practice is important.

In conversations, bring up how they can support you—do you want them to be a sounding board, do you wish them to mentor you, do you wish they use their network to serve you in some way or do you just want them to take on administrative tasks? Clear specific requests and ideas for action are the way forward.

With the Active ally, there is little needed in terms of education and ideas as they are already primed to be on your side. Active men promote and support women publicly. They make space for your aspirations and utilize their connections to open doors. Make requests on how to showcase you perhaps even outside your organization.

The Advocate ally is a full convert as they routinely champion for women, diversity and are most often men who have the feminine principles of leading well—entrenched in their leadership style. All we need to do is prompt these allys, find gratitude for their generosity and appreciate their efforts.

Women have often asked me who makes a good ally? I suggest you look at peers or a superior who has women on their team already, appears to support them and create opportunities for them and above all a person who does not show any signs of insecurity around talented women. They are typically people with respectful conversational skills and who place trust in competence above all else.

So do you have allies in your work or at home? Make a list of men you can make requests to. Go ahead and nurture those connections as they power your Step Up journey.

Self-care Is Self-love

Self-care is something that everyone knows about, speaks about but we may not do much about.

I define

**self-care as any practice that slows us down for rest or reju-
venates us while nurturing us. Self-care is that which enables
us to fulfil our promises and take care of what we care about.**

Nature has rhythms—night and day, seasons that come and go,
and the moon cycles. Our body has rhythms too—sleep,
menstruation and our heart beat. Each rhythm allows an ebb and
a flow, a high and a low, a period of action and then of rest. Each
point in time in these cycles has a distinct quality to it.

Self-care rhythms and practices enrich our lives with these same
patterns of action, rest, reflection and rejuvenation.

If you look up self-care on the Internet, I am sure you will find a
load of material to guide you. On my online Facebook group Lead
Powerful Live Mindful, I did a few events which were seen by a
few hundred members of the group. One was a two-week self-care
challenge offering 10 challenges for women and the other a seven-
day event on creating a good life. The ideas below are a distillation
of those two events as well as a pointing out the most prevalent
patterns amongst women leaders that need attention.

Self-care Rhythms and Practices

1. **Body, mind, soul care**

   The body is the vehicle that allows us to take care of what we care
   about. The mind holds our aspirations, nurtures powerful thoughts
   and dreams. Both the mind and the body need attending to. After
   a period of doing there needs to be a period of rest or downtime.
   So many spiritual traditions support this idea for the power it
   holds for us humans. Rest and rejuvenation is vital nurturing for
   ourselves.

Sleeping, eating healthy, daily exercise, meditation, mindfulness practices, reflective pauses each day, spiritual practices, hobbies, time with nature and praying are some ideas for body, mind and soul. I do a bunch of these every week and I keep working on building my muscle in this area!

2. Defining your Good Life

The idea of a 'Good Life' (1) has become a compass of sorts for me. My Good Life includes my cares. I invite you to define what is a Good Life for you at this stage in your life. This definition keeps changing and needs revisiting each year. It starts with the question: What is a Good Life for me?

Many of us are obsessed with building a career or a business and life passes us by. Many women especially live only in two dimensions—work and family. Making a definition of a Good Life is the foundation of self-care as it enables us to make choices that matter to us. Apart from work life we make time for what we have included in our overall definition of a Good Life.

The Good Life tells me who to associate with and make time for, it tells me how much is 'enough' work and what to cancel from my calendar while some days the inner voice tell me to rest or drop projects. At times it tells me I need to make a bold declaration as it serves my Good Life.

Some of our Good Life ideas might include moving away from toxic relationships, developing a healthy attitude to money and creating financial abundance. It may include becoming a farmer again or it might include a socially relevant project, travelling each year with those who are fun to be with, learning a new skill or doing a spiritual journey or course.

3. Be a goddess

Each of us have just one mind, heart and two hands that carry out tasks. Indian goddesses have many heads and many hands, hence I use the metaphor. As women who are stepping up, we need to enrol and if needed hire enough minds, hearts and hands to support us in taking care of what we care about. Notice I am not saying just extra hands. Hiring good help means you have good hearts and good minds too as they understand what you care about. Be it house help, enrolling kind and generous neighbours, extended family and service providers to whom we can outsource and delegate the more routine tasks connected with running a home, children chores or elderly care.

By all means be involved and do things when you can do them and always have the backup of other minds, good hearts and reliable hands whose help you take to take care of what you care about. Invest and nurture these individuals for they power you in invaluable ways.

4. **Network of support**

A network of support is a web that holds us, and keeps us safe, enabled and strong. Support is typically immediate family, extended family, friends, colleagues and neighbours. A support web takes effort and nurturing. It means it is mutual and we are present for them as they are for us. In times of crisis or challenge, this is invaluable as it holds us and those we love in a safety net.

Apart from my family who love me and are so proud of what I do, I have three support webs apart from them. One is a groups of friends who are therapists and facilitators like me. We share, celebrate, have fun, and share a deep language of understanding and love. It is a place I can be myself and ask for whatever I need. The second network is a group of coaches and professional colleagues who hold space if I have a personal share or a professional dilemma, or I may ask for some professional inputs or direction. We learn together, support each other's promises and cares, and do projects together. They are both a personal and professional lifeline. The third web is a group of family friends who really know how to enjoy life and celebrate. They are people who are a call away and really have my back!

I have presented many ideas for support webs here. Choose what fits you and actively bring it into your life!

Some of the lines in this poem has inspired me to show up and I share it here with you with the hope that you are inspired to show up in your Step Up journey!

Let Your Light Shine

Our deepest fear is not that we are inadequate.
Our deepest fear is that we are powerful beyond measure.
It is our light, not our darkness, that most frightens us.
We ask ourselves, who am I to be brilliant,
gorgeous, talented, fabulous?
Actually, who are you not to be?
You are a child of God.
Your playing small does not serve the world.
There is nothing enlightened about shrinking so that other
people won't feel insecure around you.
We were born to make manifest the glory of God that is
within us.
It is not just in some of us, it is in everyone.
And as we let our own light shine, we unconsciously give
other people permission to do the same.
As we are liberated from our own fear, our presence
automatically liberates others.
—Marianne Williamson

Reference

1. Brown Jennifer. *Allyship in 2018: Activating your ally voice*, https://jennifer brownspeaks.com/2018/01/12/allyship-in-2018-activating-your-ally-voice/

About the Author

Sailaja Manacha is a psychologist, psychotherapist and leadership coach. Her commitment is to develop women in leadership at all levels so that women function with agency and become designers of their life and work. Her belief is that the world today is in immense need of the feminine energy and that women need to show up as a potent and powerful presence—be it in organizations, society or in family life.

Her work is a blend of psychology, awareness-based practices and practical aspects of management and leadership learning. The same approach is applied to her women in leadership interventions as she sees the significance of bringing the gender lens to leading.

In the corporate world, she engages individuals, groups and management teams that seek mastery in powerful living, a deeper personal awareness and leadership impact that produce sustainable results. She has facilitated thousands of training and coaching programmes both public and within organizations. Her clients include Siemens STS, Cerner Healthcare India, Infosys, Firstsource, Weir Minerals, Honeywell Software, Bally Technologies, Huawei Technologies, Adobe, Kwench and many more.

She is the founder of Step Up—a 100 per cent online women leadership course launched in March 2018. She also runs an online community of emerging professional women leaders called Lead Powerful Live Mindful. The platform has exclusive and free content she curates and creates.

Within her commitment to emotional wellness and mental health in India, she runs her independent training course for psychotherapists who wish to be qualified and internationally credentialed.

She is credentialed at the highest level as a TSTA from the International Transactional Analysis Association, USA. She has been a significant contributor to the South Asian Transactional Analysis Association—a regional body of TA. Being in this field of personal transformations for over 20 years, she continues to teach TA-based public programmes.

She has a Master's in Psychology and Organizational Behaviour with over 10 years of corporate HR experience. She is an accredited coach (PCC) from the International Coach Federation (ICF) and an accredited psychotherapist. She is a Master Practitioner of Neuro-Linguistics Programming (NLP) and has trained in Germany to be a facilitator of Systemic Constellations.

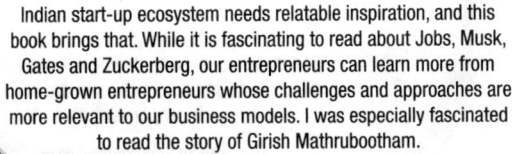